B.C.

SERMONS IN ACCENTS

OR

STUDIES IN THE HEBREW TEXT

A BOOK FOR PREACHERS AND STUDENTS

BY

REV. JOHN ADAMS, B.D.

Inverkeilor

AUTHOR OF "KINGLESS FOLK," "THE MOSAIC TABERNACLE"
"THE MINOR PROPHETS"

EDINBURGH

T. & T. CLARK, 38 GEORGE STREET

1906

THE ABERDEEN UNIVERSITY PRESS LIMITED

PREFACE

THE aim of the present volume is to furnish a readable yet sufficiently accurate account of Hebrew Accentuation. It is an attempt, however imperfect, to illustrate to others, what the author has found in his own experience, that a working knowledge of accentual law no less than of Hebrew Syntax or of Septuagint Greek can frequently be turned to good account in the practical work of preaching. Hence the choice of the main title, " Sermons in Accents ". The phrase does not mean that the outstanding feature of the book is homiletical or expository. It suggests simply that the subject has been treated from the standpoint of the preacher, and that the technical results thus won at the desk can readily be utilised in the service of the pulpit. The expository outline, in a word, is not the essential feature of the work; it is merely the spice to make it palatable.

The sub-title, " Studies in the Hebrew Text," is slightly more ambitious. It expresses the conviction that the preaching of the present is needing infused into it rather more of the Biblical element. It does not savour, as Scottish preaching used to do, of an intimate familiarity with the written word. In truth, we are reading too much about the Bible, and too little *in* it. Not, indeed, that one has any desire to revive the naïve literalness of the handy concordance plan. That method is dead and cannot be revived. The term " faith," for instance, in Hab. ii. 4 does not mean the same thing as in Gal. iii. 11 ; and it serves no good purpose to write and preach as if it did. Biblical preaching means the preaching that is based on Biblical Theology, and this in turn presupposes a first-hand acquaintance with the text. But how is this to be attained? How is the modern preacher to make sure that he is retailing week by week the fully verified results of Biblical exegesis ? Only in one way : he must get back to the ordinary Hebrew sources and verify the results for himself. If the cause of truth is to be safeguarded from the extravagance of ἀγνωσία, the preacher of the future must sit down and grapple with the minutiæ of the text.[1]

[1] If we mistake not, this is the one weakness in Dr. Orr's comprehensive and painstaking volume, *The Problem of the Old Testament*. One may read it from cover to cover

It is to this twofold service that the present work is dedicated. It seeks to go back to the Hebrew sources, yet keeps in view the practical bearing of the subject—not souring the mind by unnecessary technicalities, but introducing as much of accentual and syntactical law as to whet the desire of the average student to know more. The measure of success which has attended these efforts must of course be appraised by others ; nevertheless the following statement by one who has made a special study of the subject, and who has read the volume in MS., may fitly close this prefatory note : " I have looked through your MS. and have read enough to show me (1) that you have well mastered the technical details involved, and (2) that you have succeeded admirably in making a clear and what one might call 'popular' presentation of these details. (3) Your exhibition in each chapter of a text to be treated homiletically on the basis

and never once feel the necessity of turning up a single Hebrew word. This is a grave, if not a fatal, flaw. The psychological moment may have arrived for leading a strong reaction against the prevailing school of Old Testament criticism ; but if so it will have to be inaugurated and pressed home along another and very different line of attack. It will begin in the regular work of the Hebrew class, when the average student has been taught to prize and put to practical use the ordinary Masoretic Text.

of the accents is very happy in conception and in execution; it clinches your argument in a forcible and impressive manner. I cannot but commend your diligence in working your subject and your ready style in presenting the fruits of your labours. I should hope that there are a sufficient number of our students of divinity and young ministers so much in earnest in the study of the Old Testament Scripture that your book would receive adequate recognition and acceptance."

NOTE.—To meet the needs of the Hebrew student, a few blank pages have been inserted throughout the volume. Additional examples will constantly be met with in the course of his Hebrew studies; and if he has got into the habit of noting these under their respective sections, the inserted leaves may become, not simply a record of his reading, but a valuable addition to the present text-book. (*Cf.* p. 91, etc.)

CONTENTS

CHAPTER I

CHAPTER II

CHAPTER III

CHAPTER IV

CHAPTER V

CHAPTER VI

CHAPTER I

INTRODUCTION

THE late Professor Davidson's *Outlines of Hebrew Accentuation* appeared as early as 1861, and the flavour of the opening paragraph is delicious. "Buxtorf, the younger, when introducing a quarto of nearly five hundred pages on the accents and vowels, gracefully apologises for making so much noise about the *point*, to which the children of the mathematicians deny all magnitude. Some people may think any labour bestowed upon the accents ill-spent. But surely no labour is ill-spent which is spent upon the text of Scripture. And it must not be forgotten that accents and vowels are of the same authority, both having sprung entire from the head of the Masorete, and whoso condemns the one condemns the other. No doubt those whose condemnation falls so ruinously upon the accents would dispense with the vowels as well. Would many of them feel the loss of *dispensing with the consonants also?*"

1

Probably not: and yet from another point of view they might have a desire to retain them in their service. The consonants are not unlike Sherlock Holmes' dancing men. You can move them about and re-arrange them in all conceivable combinations, until they mean anything or nothing; and it would be a most serious loss to those of us who occasionally engage in this pastime, if there were no men left to dance. The accents and vowels, which form a kind of bodyguard around the Masoretic text, may be cut down without a pang in the fight for a purer standard; but it is obvious that the consonants occupy a slightly different position: one must leave something to fight about. And for his part, the present writer has no wish to see the fighting cease. He holds no brief to defend either the accents or the consonants. If the other criteria demand it, the consonantal text itself, no less than the dual system of punctuation, must give place to a more satisfactory reconstruction of the Hebrew original. Indeed, in several of the examples adduced in the following pages this right of textual emendation as applied to the entire Masoretic material is frankly recognised and acted upon. We can have no hesitation in endorsing the conclusion of Canon Driver, that to some extent, at least, the study of Hebrew Grammar has been artificially complicated by a corrupt text. "In some cases it is only the vocalisation, in others it is the consonantal text itself which appears to be at fault." [1] But what then? The first duty of the student or of the preacher is *not* to get behind the Masoretic text, but to get back to the Hebrew text *as we have it*—to sift its history, weigh its problems, admire its diction, and assimilate its thought, and above all to use it week by week in the practical work of the ministry. For only then is he in a position to appreciate the labours of those who would lead him into the further field of textual emendation; or what is of deeper interest, only then will he find in his pulpit preparation that expository preaching is an inspiration and a joy.

1. THE VALUE OF THE ACCENTS

Historically and even exegetically the study of the accents needs no apology. They were part of the means adopted by the Masoretes for preserving the pronunciation of the text and the intonation of the Synagogue; and while they were essentially a musical system, they are frequently found to be of real service both in the sphere of grammar and of exegesis. "Some acquaintance with accents is indispensable to the

[1] *Hebrew Tenses*, p. viii.

Hebrew student," says Canon Driver, "not only
for the single object, with a view to which this
account of them has been inserted here, but upon
more general grounds as well; they frequently
offer material assistance in unravelling the sense
of a difficult passage; and the best authorities
continually appeal to them, on account of their
bearing upon exegesis. Experience tells me how
liable they are to be overlooked; and the object
of the present chapter is merely to smooth the
way for those who may desire to pursue the subject more thoroughly afterwards, or, for such as
have not the time or inclination to do this, to lay
down a few broad rules which may be of practical
service." [1]

Words are sometimes distinguished by the
accents alone, as *'ó-ri* "shine" (Isa. lx. 1), and
'o-rí "my light" (Ps. xxvii. 1), just as in Greek
we have εἰμί and εἶμι, and in English, présent and
presént. Similarly in Isa. liii. 7, we have a form
of the verb which is either a *perfect* or a *participle*, according as we print it נָאֱלָ֫מָה (with
Baer) or נֶאֱלָ֫מָה (with Ginsburg).

For the preacher, however, the main plea in
behalf of a more accurate study of Hebrew accents
has yet to be mentioned. They form part of a

---

[1] *Hebrew Tenses*, p. 101.

preacher's apparatus in the practical work of exposition. The way in which a passage is arranged
accentually is sometimes the one hint necessary
for suggesting a suitable division of the subject.
There are sermons in accents. It may not be the
first object of the present volume to show how
sermons are to be found; but we confidently
assure the hard-driven sermon-maker that even
from this point of view, he will not read through
the following pages in vain. We offer him a full
sheaf of expository outlines with ample sugges-
tions as to where he can find more.

Let him open, for instance, the Hebrew Bible
at Gen. i. 1, and note the marvellous accuracy of
the Masoretic notation. A considerable pause
is placed on the first word, according to the rule
that prepositions with their government at the
beginning of a clause are generally marked off
by a disjunctive accent. This was the time when,
and the place where, the great Artificer began
the mighty task. "*In the beginning*—God created the heaven and the earth." The main pause,
however, is placed on "Elohim," not simply for
the sake of musical equilibrium, but because this
is the one thought that illumines everything. The
worker is always greater than his work. "In
the beginning—*God created !* the heaven and the
earth." Finally, there are two stages in the work

and two beats in the music—the heaven first
(as it ought to be) and the earth in subordination to it, and therefore both separated by
a disjunctive accent, but wrought also into a
finished whole (a cosmos) by the final dominating pause Silluq. So that the divisions of our
subject are lying on the surface :—

      (1) The Time when,

      (2) The Worker,

      (3) The Work,

—an arrangement which may be represented
to eye and ear alike by being printed and read
thus :—

> In the beginning—*God* created !
> The heaven, and the earth.

Or the student may turn to one of the pro-
phetical writings and read as in Hab. i. 1 :—

> The burden which he saw,
> Habakkuk the prophet.

This is the order of the words as given in the
Hebrew, and the subject-matter as thus arranged
is full of interest for the preacher. The chief
pause is placed on " saw," not simply to conserve
the balance of the sentence, but because, in the
estimation of the punctuator, " the vision and the
faculty divine " was even more important than
the thing revealed. This is the condition of all
true prophesying in the name of the Lord. The
prophet must be a *seer* or rapt gazer in the audi-

ence-chamber of Jehovah. Was it not so in the
case of the great Exemplar? "In the beginning
was the Word, and the Word was *with* God"
(πρὸς τὸν Θεόν). He was in the presence of, and
ever turning *towards* (πρός) the central Majesty.
In Godet's fine language, "To reveal God, one
must know Him: to project Him outwardly one
must have plunged into His bosom. The character of revealer is therefore subordinate, even in
the Logos, to a personal communion with God.
He contemplates before reflecting, He receives
before giving." On the other hand the genuine
prophet does reflect. He is *Nabî* no less than
Chozeh. He has a message to deliver to the men
of his own generation. And therefore a second
fairly strong pause is placed on "burden," the
oracle or substance of Habakkuk's message. It
is not to be true of him that "strongest minds are
often those of whom the noisy world hears least".
He has the inspired utterance no less than the
open vision, the "accomplishment of verse," no
less than the faculty divine: and it is his to turn
round as the Lord's mouthpiece to speak to men
what he has seen and heard. Hence a suitable
division of our text would be :—

(1) The method of revelation (חָזָה).

(2) The substance of revelation (הַמַּשָּׂא).

(3) The personal recipient (הֲבַקּוּק).

2. LITERATURE

The student is sometimes advised to sell his Hebrew Bible, and buy the works of some worthy Puritan, who, as a modern preacher has discovered, has thoughts that breathe and words that burn like any other accepted author. We strongly urge him to do nothing of the kind. Those saintly men of a by-gone age did a splendid work in their own time, and we who have been enriched by their labours most gratefully revere their memory. But like the systems they represented, they have had their day and ceased to be; and the duty laid upon the new generation is not to sell the text-book of the Christian ministry, and go and purchase weapons that are fast becoming antiquated; but to enter the armoury from which these were supplied and find suitable weapons for ourselves. If any books must be sold, let it be anything rather than the Hebrew Bible. Let it be the Puritans themselves which are relegated to the shelves of the second-hand bookseller, if by any means their vacated places may be filled by the following *apparatus criticus* :—

(1) *The Baer and Delitzsch Texts*, as far at least as these have been published—Exodus, Leviticus, Numbers and Deuteronomy have not as yet appeared. These should be bound separately and

interleaved, and while the student is still conversant with his Latin, a literal translation of the Introductions and Notes should be inscribed on the inserted leaves of each volume—a task which will form a splendid preparation for the subsequent study of the text.

(2) Ginsburg's *Introduction* to the Hebrew Bible—a volume which is not only requisite for his own edition of the text, but has placed all Hebrew students under a debt of gratitude to the painstaking editor.

(3) Wickes' standard work on the *Hebrew Accents*. This consists of two companion treatises which appeared in 1881 and 1887 respectively—the former dealing with the three so-called poetical books of the old Testament, and the latter with the twenty-one so-called prose books. For any one who desires to pursue the subject of Hebrew accents further, these two treatises are indispensable. Without them the present volume would never have been written.

(4) *The Old Testament in Greek*, or Swete's edition of the Septuagint.[1] Its short but scholarly introductions will furnish the student with the necessary point of view for profiting by the various MS. readings grouped at the foot of each

[1] See additional note, p. 13.

page. This "manual" edition is the best, as it
is the latest of all the Septuagints.

(5) Hatch's *Essays* in Biblical Greek. As a
guide to the language of the LXX, and an introduction to some of its problems, this volume can
be thoroughly recommended to the Old Testament student. It is a work of sterling value
and well worth the time one may spend upon it.

(6) The following *Articles* in our new Bible
Dictionaries should also be carefully studied.
Nestle's excellent contribution on the "Septua-
gint," and Strack's equally fine handling of the
"Text of the Old Testament" in Hastings' *Bible
Dictionary;* with F. C. Burkitt's "Text and
Versions" in the *Encyclopædia Biblica.*

But the main item in the student's working
apparatus has yet to be noted. He should prepare a critical edition of certain portions of the
Hebrew text for himself. To his other purchases
he should add a dozen large note-books suitable for this purpose; and when he has an evening to spare he should address himself to the
task of arrangement and pagination. Let him
assign to each verse in the selected portion the
two pages which face one another in the pre-
viously arranged note-book. He may read, for
instance, in Cheyne's admirable article on "Job"
in the *Biblica* that the opening words in vii. 20.

ought to be omitted as an interpolation: and as this happens to occur in one of the sections which he has set apart for special study, he turns up the page referred to and makes a note of the suggested emendation. He transcribes the Hebrew at the top of the left-hand page, and the rendering of the LXX at the top of the page opposite; and then comparing the two, he inserts the note in the space beneath. Nothing more may be added on this particular passage for some considerable time: but gradually in the course of his reading, one note after another finds its way into the allotted space, until at the close of several years of study it may read as at page 192 in the appendix. In this way the student has constructed for himself the best Index Rerum in the market. He has devised an efficient method for keeping a record of his reading, and is gradually producing a critical edition of the text—a work which to him, at least, will be in after years the most valuable book in his library.

3. Our Motto

Our motto, then, is "back to the Hebrew text". It is not enough to browse through various magazine articles, and retail at second or even at third hand the facts or fancies of others. We must get back to the ordinary Hebrew sources and verify the results for ourselves. If need be, we must copy the devotion of the old Rabbis who did not scruple to burn the midnight oil in the prosecution of their studies. "Hananiah ben Hezekiah," says the Babylonian Talmud, " is of blessed memory, for but for him Ezekiel would have been declared apocryphal, because his words contradicted the words of the Law : *three hundred jars of lamp oil were brought to him, and he sat in his garret and solved the contradictions.*" That is his example to Hebrew students to-day. Let them toil as he did at their Old Testament tasks. And they shall yet know something of the beauty of the language and the loftiness of the thought, when they have learned

> To scorn delights, and live laborious days.

A "larger" edition of *The Old Testament in Greek* is now announced. It differs from the smaller or manual edition in providing a more extended *apparatus criticus*. But since "the result confirms the substantial accuracy of the manual edition," the expositor will find, both in price and various readings, that the smaller work is sufficiently comprehensive for his purpose.

CHAPTER II

THE ACCENTUATORS

THE accents and vowels were introduced into the Hebrew Scriptures about the seventh century A.D. As this, however, is part of a larger question dealing with the preservation and history of the text, it may help us to appreciate the distinctive labours of the accentuators, if we cast a glance, however summary, at the previous history of the Sopherim. Indeed, the three main landmarks in this wider field of inquiry correspond to the three names—Sopherim, Masoretes and Punctuators; and in order to place our subject in its proper historical setting, we may profitably assign one short section to each.

1. THE SOPHERIM

A large part of the consonantal text was probably in existence by the time of Ezra. The book of the "Law" especially, was the valued possession and accepted guide of the post-exilian church (Ezra vii. 6, Neh. viii. 1). But possession is only one thing. The revision of the text, and

its careful preservation against possible sources
of corruption, was no less a service demanded by
the Church of God, and a task to which the ablest
scholars of the age might well apply their energies.
It was this service that was undertaken by the
Sopherim or scribes. They were the doctors and
authorised interpreters of the Law, who, during
the last centuries B.C. and at the beginning of the
Christian era, toiled patiently at the "hedge"
which was designed henceforth to enclose and
preserve the sacred consonantal text. According to the Talmud they were called Sopherim
(סוֹפְרִים = γραμματεῖς) or "counters," because they
counted all the letters and words in the various
Hebrew documents. "Thus they said that the
vav in גחון (Lev. xi. 42), is the middle letter in
the Pentateuch, that דרש דרש (Lev. x. 16) is
the middle word, that Lev. xiii. 33 is the middle
verse, that the ע in מיער (Ps. lxxx. 14) is the
middle letter in the Psalter, and that Ps. lxxviii.
36 is the middle verse." [1]

But the fullest statement, respecting their
activity and functions, is found in the Babylonian Talmud. We are there informed that the
Sopherim fixed the pronunciation of words,

[1] See Ginsburg's Introduction, p. 69, which also gives the
original.

indicated various instances where *vav* conjunctive ought to be cancelled, specified a number of
words which though not written are to be read,
and *vice versâ*, words which though present in
the text, are nevertheless to be omitted in the
reading — and then follows a list of examples
illustrative of each.[1] The whole passage suggests
that the Sopherim were not merely copyists of
the sacred writings but revisers and redactors;
and other evidence which may be culled from
the LXX and from the Masorah points in the
same direction. In fine, they did not scruple
to exercise the right of textual emendation. A
large part of their work consisted in removing
indelicate expressions, anthropomorphisms, pro-
fane phrases towards the Deity, the too frequent
use of the Tetragrammaton—everything, in a
word, which was calculated to offend pious souls
when the sacred text was being read in the worship of the Synagogue. They winced, for instance, at the expression in 1 Sam. iii. 13 that
the sons of Eli had cursed or spoken against
God (אלהים, LXX θεόν), or the analogous
allusion in Job vii. 20 where the patriarch
expostulates saying, "Why hast thou set me as
a mark for thee, so that I am a burden to *thee*?"

[1] Ginsburg, p. 308.

2

(עָלֶיךָ, LXX ἐπὶ σοί). These and similar expressions seemed to contain too bold a statement when applied to the Holy One of Israel; and therefore the words were emended by this guild of scholars, so as to convey a meaning that was less derogatory to the Deity. The term אֱלֹהִים was changed to לָהֶם, and עָלֶיךָ to עָלַי, and then the passages read as in the R.V. that Eli's sons "did bring a curse upon *themselves*" and that Job said, "So that I am a burden to *myself*".

But however extensive and thorough the work of the Sopherim may have been, it practically came to an end in the first century of our era. They had patiently sought to edit and preserve the sacred Hebrew writings, and so well had they succeeded in their efforts that the text we now possess, so far as the consonants are concerned, is substantially the same as that settled by these authoritative redactors. The extant Hebrew MSS. certainly give the consonants with great fidelity. Throughout the forty-eight chapters of Ezekiel, for instance, only sixteen real variations occur between a modern edition, based on Western MSS. and the St. Petersburg Codex of the Prophets, a recently discovered MS. of wholly eastern ancestry. Whatever may have been the case before the Christian era, very few changes have been allowed since then to creep into the Hebrew text. So that the work of the Sopherim is still possessed by the Church in much the same form as it left the redactors' hands. The consonantal text was now finally settled, and passed over at the beginning of the Christian era into the safe keeping of

2. THE MASORETES

If it was the signal glory of the Sopherim to revise and finally settle the consonants of the Hebrew text, a similar honour fell to the lot of the Masoretes in introducing and perfecting the dual system of punctuation. They bequeathed to their successors a system of vowels and accents so complete, that it has preserved for all time the traditional pronunciation and musical recitation of the Synagogue. They were led to this invention by the exigencies of their position. So long as Hebrew was a living speech, the need was not felt of devising a system of visible vocalisation. The consonants themselves provided a rough sketch of the language, and warmth and colour, *i.e.*, the vowels and accents, could always be added from an intimate acquaintance with the vernacular and a familiar knowledge of the context. It was only when classical Hebrew was supplanted by Aramaic as the language of com-

mon life, and when Aramaic, in turn, gave place
to Arabic as the result of the Mohammedan con-
quest, that Jewish scholars felt that the task
could no longer be evaded—the pronunciation
and accentuation of their sacred books must be
fixed and represented by suitable graphical signs.

The precise date at which these signs were introduced cannot be determined with certainty.
It may be fixed anywhere between the fifth and
the eighth century A.D. It is not probable that
the system sprang fully formed from the head of
the Masorete. Beginning with a freer use of the
vowel letters — the so-called *matres lectiones*,
אהוי—and borrowing, it may be, the diacritical
point by which the Syriac punctuation had already marked the chief pauses in the verse, the
Hebrew system advanced to ever higher stages
of efficiency, until at the close of the seventh
century, it became the flexible and effective instrument the punctuators found it to be. Rabbinical authorities, indeed, were inclined to view
it in a different light. Ben-Asher, who lived in
the early part of the tenth century, was of opinion
that it ought to be assigned to the Sopherim and
wise men who with Ezra at their head were sup-
posed to have constituted the Great Synagogue.
Others, with unique courage, were prepared to
carry it a step further. They regarded it as coeval

with the language itself and communicated to Adam in Paradise! But the silence of the Talmud on the subject of the punctuation, and Jerome's express testimony that neither vowels nor accents were found in the texts of his day, have long since satisfied scholars that it cannot have been *earlier* than the fifth century. Wickes is equally convinced that it could not have been *later* than the seventh. Direct historical notices fail us altogether, but we have various considerations that seem to point to this conclusion. Ben-Asher's opinion, already referred to, shows that in his age, the origin of the system was lost in obscurity. They knew as little about it as we do. But obviously a system, the origin of which is shrouded in the mists of the past, must be of much older date than the age in question. Besides, Ben-Asher himself was the last of a distinguished family of Masoretes and punctuators whose genealogy can be traced back through five generations up to the latter half of the eighth century. It follows that the scheme of accents and vowels at which they laboured in succession must be older than the year 775, the date of their illustrious sire—Asher הזקן הגדול. These and similar considerations point to the close of the seventh century as the most probable date for the origin of the system. And if we bear in mind

that the same period synchronises with the perfecting of similar systems in the Syriac and
Greek Churches, it may not seem so improbable
an assumption after all. The age in large measure
is a *terra incognita* to the Hebrew student; but
looking before and after, a general outline of the
Masoretes' activity is not difficult to follow. They
had accepted at the beginning the charge of the
consonantal text ; and now a complete system of
interpunction and musical notation having been
wrought into its structure, they were handing it
down combined with an extensive apparatus of
other Masoretic material into the safe keeping of
a third guild of scholars—the producers of all the
extant Hebrew MSS., *viz. :*—

3. The Punctuators

Unlike the Masoretes who had to invent the
graphical signs, the functions of the punctuators
were not to create, but simply to preserve the
Masoretic labours. A glance at the facsimile of
a Hebrew MS. like that shown at p. 625 of
Ginsburg's Introduction, will help to indicate
the extent of these labours, as well as the
efficient way in which those painstaking scholars
set about their task. In addition to the vowels
and accents inserted in the text, there were also
numerous Masoretic notes inscribed in the mar-

gin. Some of these notes refer to anomalies of
vocalisation, or enumerate the various readings
of the *Q'ri* and *K'thibh*. Others indicate the
number of times certain words occur, as ב
= twice, and קלד = 134 times. Since these,
however, are frequently elaborated into the figures
of plants, animals, and other designs, the precise
meaning of the annotation is not always easy
to decipher. The brief and separate remarks
found in the side margins of our copies are
grouped under the common title, *Masorah parva*.
The longer lists, with citation of passages, inserted in the top and bottom margins of the
same page are the *Masorah magna*. But as
some of these larger lists were too lengthy for
the margins of the page on which one of the
peculiarities occurs, the Masoretes appended a
considerable number of them at the end of
different MSS. under the name *Masorah finalis*,
the whole series forming part of that vast
system of "marginal references" by which those
earnest toilers at "the hedge" sought to preserve
the integrity of the Masoretic standard.

With this material lying before him, it was
the first duty of the punctuator to furnish for
his own use a *model codex* of the Scripture.
This he did in accordance with the Masorah ;

compiling at the same time an independent
collection of Masoretic rubrics to be used, as
occasion offered, in the course of his professional
labours. The first scholars who have produced
such standard codices, and whose date we know,
are the two Ben-Ashers, father and son, who
laboured at Tiberias, and Ben-Naphtali, who
flourished in Babylonia (*cir.* 890-940). Ben-
Asher the younger, who has the credit of having
fixed the pronunciation as we have it in our
texts, was the compiler of a codex which still
exists in the Jewish community of Aleppo. Ben-
Naphtali, on the contrary, his textual rival, is
known simply from the official lists which, trans-
mitted to us in different MSS., exhibit the variations of these two rival critics.

The preparation of an ordinary Hebrew MS.
is not difficult to follow. A copyist having been
employed to produce a copy of the consonantal
text, the punctuator sat down and revised it in
the light of his model codex. And having satisfied himself that the work was sufficiently well
done, he furnished it with the Masoretic vowel-
signs and accents, and added as much of the
Masorahs, parva and magna, as the necessities of
the case seemed to demand. The extent of these
observations was regulated by various considerations, by the space available, by the inclin-

ation of the punctuator, and chiefly by the
honorarium offered by the man who ordered the
copy. In this way the majority of our Hebrew
MSS. came into existence. They were produced
by professional punctuators who, induced by the
terms offered by some wealthy patron, had undertaken the work.

But the activity of these critics was not con-
fined to the production of such MSS. If they
continued to conserve the labours of the older
Masoretes, they also led the way to the later
theorists and grammarians. They composed
treatises on the vocalic and accentual systems,
and explained the rules of the Masorah. Allusion may be made to the treatise called in some
MSS. *Dikdukē Ha-Teamim,* or " The Grammar of
the Accents ". It was first published in the
Editio Princeps of the Rabbinical Bible by Felix
Pratensis (Venice, 1517), where it is described in
the heading as the compilation of Rabbi Ben-
Asher. But despite the labours of Baer and
Strack (Leipzig, 1879), Ginsburg does not believe
that Ben-Asher had anything to do with it.
The rubrics therein contained represent portions
of the Masorah which have been gradually
developed from a period much earlier than Ben-
Asher to a time much later than this textual
critic. So that instead of the independent

treatise which its latest editors imagine it to have been, it is probably nothing more than a collection of sundry precepts and opinions propounded by different Masoretic schools. Be this as it may, the book is confessedly a product of the age when the principles of the Masorah were giving place to the ingenious speculations of later theorists. It may therefore be taken as an indication that the long-continued labours of the Masoretes were now approaching completion, and that the history of the text, as a subject of further investigation, had entered the sphere of the grammarian.[1]

4. A Practical Illustration

Allusion has been made to the *Tiqqunim* or emendations of the scribes, and the preacher will find a noteworthy example at Hab. i. 12. According to the present Masoretic text and accents the whole verse may be arranged in the form of a tetrastich :—

> Art not thou from everlasting ?
> O Lord my God, mine Holy One, we shall not die:
> O Lord, thou hast ordained him for judgment ;
> And thou, O Rock, hast established him for correction.

But the R.V. has adopted a slightly different ar-

---

[1] In a second volume entitled *Sermons in Syntax*, the author hopes, in the near future, to continue this historical sketch.

rangement. Following the division of the LXX,
it has extended the introductory question to
" mine Holy One," and placed the dichotomy
there. " Art not thou from everlasting, O Lord
my God, mine Holy One? we shall not die." The
R.V. however, has done more than this. It has
furnished the key to another matter which may
help to set the entire passage in a fresh light.
Contrary to its usual practice, it has inserted the
following note in the margin : " According to an
ancient Jewish tradition, *thou diest not*". In
other words, this is one of the emendations assigned to the Sopherim. Instead of the original
תָמוּת, which those devout scholars considered
too bold an expression to apply to the Holy One
of Israel, they introduced the 1st per. plur.
נָמוּת " *we* shall not die"; and thus taught the
deeply significant truth that God's faithful remnant can never perish. *Cf.* the similar reassuring
note in chap. ii. 4, that the righteous shall *live*
in his faithfulness.

What effect would this have on the general
arrangement of the verse, and on the accentuation
of the first couplet in particular ? With no change
of subject at "thou diest not," there would be no
necessity for placing a strong logical pause at
"mine Holy One "; and for the same reason the
punctuator would have been left with a free hand

to conserve the musical equilibrium of Athnach's clause. He would have pointed the entire couplet from Athnach as a starting-point; and thus at one stroke would have preserved the balance of the melody, the parallelism of the thought, and the deeper doctrine from which alone the immortality of the people can spring, *viz.*, the eternity and immortality of Israel's God. Thus:—

$$\text{הֲלוֹא אַתָּה מִקֶּדֶם יְהוָֹה אֱלֹהַי}$$
$$\text{קְדֹשִׁי לֹא תָמֽוּת}$$

Art not thou from everlasting, O Jehovah?
My God, mine Holy One, thou shalt not die.

The line of thought suggested by this emended text is sufficiently expressive.

1. The *eternity*, *holiness* and *immortality* of Israel's God (1st couplet).

2. The *immortality* and *ideal holiness* of Jehovah's people (2nd couplet).

And the former is the pledge of the latter. " Because I live, ye shall live also " (John xiv. 19). Not even the dreaded invasion of the Chaldeans would be for destruction, but for *correction*. Out of that furnace of affliction the faithful remnant would yet be brought an inwardly holy church. The God of their fathers was not unmindful of His covenant promise, and chastisement was but the proof of His love (*cf.* Heb. xii. 6).

For another example of the Tiqqunim of the Scribes see Hos. iv. 7. Not "*I* will change *their* glory" (כְּבוֹדָם . . . אָמִיר), but "*They* have changed *my* glory (כְּבוֹדִי הֵמִירוּ . . .) into shame". This is in perfect harmony with the context. The entire verse, like the remainder of the paragraph, deals with the unfaithfulness of the priests. They had increased in number and in prestige under Jeroboam II.; but the more they multiplied, the more they had sinned against the Lord. They had even battened upon the vices of the people. The sins were mainly these three :—

1. The forsaking of the law of God, or the neglecting of their intellectual trust (ver. 6).
2. Thriving upon the fines and sin-offerings of the worshippers, or living merrily on Israel's sin (ver. 8).
3. The outcome of both—the turning of God's glory, and therefore their own sacerdotal splendour, into shame. It required no divine act to cover them with infamy. They themselves had plunged into the abyss.

CHAPTER III

ONE's first glance at a Hebrew Bible is anything but reassuring. Instead of shedding light on a difficult and unfamiliar script, the system of notation seems only to have made confusion worse confounded by sprinkling a formidable array of points and strokes all over the text. The graphical signs are certainly complex enough ; and one is apt to conclude that the cause of Hebrew study would have been better served, if the Rabbinical scholars of vocalic and accentual lore had never really existed. Naturally the Rabbis themselves were of a different opinion. So far from increasing the difficulties of the language, they thought they were making it easier, at least for beginners. The whole scheme was devised, not simply to conserve the integrity of the consonantal text, but also to assist the laity in the correct pronunciation of the words, and especially to meet the needs of children at school. " I was not allowed to break up a Bible-verse," says R. Chananya, "except in the instruction of school-children." The Hebrew student, therefore, is not to be discouraged by his first glance at the accentual system. It was only food for babes.

1. ITS EXTRALINEAR CHARACTER

According to the Jewish view of the sacred writings, the consonants alone are to be regarded as Scripture. Even to this day nothing but the consonants are admitted into the rolls that are written out for use in the Synagogues. And therefore *a priori* no system of punctuation could be recognised, which would have involved an alteration of the traditional letters. It might take the form of a series of points and strokes, inserted below or above the Hebrew characters *i.e.*, it might be infralinear like that of the Occidentals, or superlinear like that of the Orientals, but it must not make the graphical signs appear of equal value with the old letters, not by one jot or tittle must the Hebrew consonants be displaced.

A single clause from Job xxxvi. 7 will help to illustrate this Jewish scruple.

(1) The Palestinian pointing :—

וַיּוֹשִׁיבֵם לָנֶצַח וַיִּגְבָּהוּ :

(2) The Babylonian pointing:—

וִישִׁיבֵם לָנֶצַח וַיִּגְבָּהוּ׃

The difference between these two systems lies
more in the notation than in the pronunciation ;
but both agree in this, that whatever be the time
or order of their development, they have succeeded in keeping intact the sacred consonantal
text. The question of priority is not so easily
settled. Dr. Wickes is of opinion that the palm
ought to be assigned to the Palestinian punctuation, inasmuch as the Babylonian system has all
the appearance of being an unsuccessful attempt
to improve upon the former. But Ginsburg
maintains that the two notations were developed
independently of each other ; and that it is
simply a case of special pleading to argue that
the superlinear pointing is not the product of the
Babylonian school of Masoretes. In any case
the superlinear system can be best studied in
Strack's facsimile of the St. Petersburg Codex
of the prophets of the date A.D. 916, or in a
fourth MS. of the same Firkowitsch collection,
containing the last chapters of the book of Job.
Both MSS. were brought to light some sixty
years ago by the researches of Abraham Firkowitsch, a Karaite Jew, in the synagogues of the
Crimea. A specimen page of the Job Codex

3

may be found inserted as a frontispiece to Baer's
Liber Jobi.

Notable in this system is the absence of a sign
for S'gol which is replaced by *a* or *i*. Furtive
Pathach also is entirely awanting. The signs for
the principal vowels are formed from the vowel
letters, יואַ, and the disjunctive accents, instead
of the simple marks of the Palestinian system,
are frequently represented by the initial letter
of their Hebrew names, as a diminutive ת for
T'bhir, or a mutilated ש for S'golta. In other
respects it seems to be a modification of the Arabic
system of representing the vowels—a fact which
may help to explain the position of the signs
above the letters. But while the originators of
this system avoid some of the weak points of the
Palestinian notation, as for instance, the confound-
ing of Y'thibh with M'huppakh or Pashta with
Azla, it nevertheless has been eclipsed by its
western rival, and like the Eastern recension of
the text generally, has passed out of practical use.
For one thing, it is not so simple as the infralinear system. The position of its vowel signs
above the line brings them inconveniently into
conflict with the superlinear accents. Its inability to distinguish Pathach and S'gol, and
sometimes Pathach and Qametz; or its use of the

same horizontal stroke (ˉ) to denote the different values of Raphe, vocal sheva and silent sheva, places it at a great disadvantage as compared with the infralinear pointing. And as no second method is required to compass the same task of vocalisation, the simpler and more convenient method has gradually gained the ascendency. Alike in its system of notation, and in its recension of the text, the Tiberian school of Masoretes has prevailed.

2. Its Musico-logical Character

A twofold purpose seems to have been served by the Hebrew accents. As signs of interpunction they correspond in some measure with our *stops*, indicating as these do the grammatical and syntactical divisions of the verse. Yet since the verse had also to be read, no less than written, or chanted according to a particular mode of cantillation in use at the time, the accents came to express the solemn recitation of the Synagogue, or the modulation of the living voice in the public reading of the Scripture. They combined logic and music. Obviously it is only the first element in the system that is of real consequence to us. The Jews themselves admit that its musical value has in large measure been lost. So that if we come to the subject desiring simply what is useful

or practical in the scheme, the element of music
will not bulk largely in our ultimate appreciation
of the facts. It is not as an index to musical in-
flexion, but solely as a guide to the meaning of
the text, that the study of the accents is of positive
service to the student of Biblical Hebrew.

The practical aspect, however, is not everything. Historical, and even genealogical considerations may be of equal interest in the
prosecution of such an inquiry. And if those
writers are correct, who base the whole system
in the traditional modulation of the Synagogue,
we may have to write "musico-logical," and not
vice versâ, as the fitting designation of its development. That such a modulation really
existed before the introduction of the graphical
signs is evident from the testimony of the Talmud. The tradition in *Megilla* 3ᵃ traces it back
even to the time of Ezra ; and Wickes believes
that the opinion as thus expressed may not be
so groundless as it looks. The mode of recitation may well have been one of the institutions
established soon after Ezra's time for the more
formal conduct of public worship. " From the
Temple it would pass into the Synagogue. And
perhaps Christ Himself made use of it, when
reading from the prophet Isaiah (Luke iv. 17)."

But however interesting this speculation may

be, it is the logical value of the accents that con-
stitutes their chief claim on our attention. Their
very name is an evidence of this fact. Instead
of the term נְעִימָה "melody," they are called
טְעָמִים "senses or meanings" (from טָעַם "to taste
or perceive"): that is, they are regarded as marks
of sense, or signs of logical interpunction. In
this signification, however, they are not abso-
lute like our points. They do not indicate
a complete and independent meaning like our
period. It may take several Hebrew verses to
form a complete logical period; and on the other
hand, several logical periods may be contained in
one Hebrew verse. What it does imply is that
the text was not only recited in the public worship of the Synagogue, but recited in such a way
as to bring out the meaning of the passage, and
impress it on the minds of the hearers. The rise
and fall of the modulation was to reflect the
logical and syntactical relation of the words.
Hence not only in the great pauses of the sense,
but in the finer shades of distinction that
characterise the language, the musical notation
was all that was requisite for punctuating the
text—the melody and the syntax coalesced.

The melody, then, is not to be forgotten in our
study of the accentual system. Certain except-

tional cases are not to be explained in any other
way.   For example, the greater distinctives are
sometimes found with smaller distinctives immediately before them (Hos. vi. 10), though both
logic and syntax demand a connective instead of
a distinctive; and many words appear with two
accents or sometimes as many as three (Job. vi.
10), a phenomenon which can have no reference
to logic.   These and similar anomalies are to be
explained by the musical character of the dec-
lamation.   It generally adapts itself to the logical
and grammatical laws, but if for the sake of
emphasis, or in order to preserve the particular
form of composition known as Hebrew Parallelism, it occasionally deviates from the strict rules
of syntax, this, in view of similar licences adopted
in other languages, is just what might have been
expected.   Its purely musical character is sometimes the dominating fact.

3. The Value of this Fact in the Practical Work of Translation

Hebrew accentuation is therefore something
more than our modern system of interpunction.
It is not simply the accurate division of the
written sense, but the visible representation of
the living utterance.   It is a sensuous oratory,
intended for the eye instead of the ear, and can

express shades of meaning that are far beyond the compass of our more prosaic grammatical divisions. And yet it is just these finer shades of thought and feeling that give to the careful student the highest form of mental pleasure, and repay him for all the labour he has expended in the analysis of the text. They fill him with the joy of elevated thought. The bearing of this fact on the practical work of translation cannot be over-estimated.

The following illustration, at least in substance, may be found at p. 49 of Professor Davidson's early *Outlines* : " In the house of Israel I have seen an horrible thing " (Hos. vi. 10). The translation as thus given may be accurate enough as a rendering of the unaccented Hebrew, but it is totally inadequate as a suitable expression of the Masoretic, accents. These are nothing if not emphatic, but the solemnity and dignity that ought to be attributed to them are almost entirely awanting in this rendering. The chief accent within the clause is at *Israel ;* for the speaker is represented as lingering over the sacredness of the name, as if repelled by the thought that she, the chosen nation, could have been guilty of such a deed ! Then with a second fairly strong pause at *seen*, which we can only represent by a dash or similar device, the devout reader hesitates once more, as if afraid to utter the last solemn word—*an horrible thing*. So that in order to bring out the meaning of the living utterance, we must render in some such manner as the following:—

> In the house of *Israel!*
> I have seen—an horrible thing.

The general sense is obvious enough even in our English version, but who does not feel that the meaning is greatly enriched by an intelligent appreciation of the Masoretic notation?

It is granted, of course, that what we are now dealing with in the accentual system is simply the meaning of the text as understood by the Masoretes. And since it frequently resolves itself into a mere matter of taste as to what feeling or emphasis ought to be read into each passage, we may not always be able to agree with their judgment. Even in this case, however, we are not to do injustice to the value of their general conclusions. They belonged to a time when the idiom of the language was still a living speech; and they were consequently in a better position for appraising the truth in this matter than any subsequent toilers in the field of Biblical exegesis. They may not have supplied in every case a satisfactory rendering of the logical and syntactical divisions, but in repeated instances they have succeeded in fixing the sense in a far more effective way than our modern system of interpunction. Turn, for instance, to Ps. xxxviii. 12.

> They also that seek after my life lay snares for me ;
> And they that seek my hurt speak mischievous things,
> And imagine deceits all the day long.

Professor Duhm suggests another grouping of the clauses in this verse. By supplying עָלַי after רָעָתִי which may easily have fallen out on account of the similarity, he would place the main logical pause at "hurt," and arrange the whole verse as a distich, consisting of two fairly equal and parallel lines.

> And they lay snares, who plot for my life and seek after my hurt :
> And they speak evil (against me) and murmur deceit all the day long.

Yet in no wise is this an improvement on the generally accepted division. Not only is it at variance with the LXX, and with the Hebrew accents, but it obliterates the plain threefold division in the advance of the thought. The first two lines form an exact parallelism, dealing with hostility in *act* and hostility in *speech*—the main distinctive accent being retained to mark the close of both ; and then a third member is added, dealing with hostility in *motive*, either as an expansion of the second line in the parellelism, or as the necessary explanation of the whole. It is the former of these alternatives which is suggested by the English punctuation, but the Hebrew accents are in favour of the latter. And there can be no question that the Hebrew pointing is correct. Beneath the outward hostility of violence and calumny is found the inward plotting of deceit.

On the other hand, Mal. iii. 17 is an instance where the Hebrew student may feel justified in exercising his own judgment, אֲשֶׁר אֲנִי עֹשֶׂה סְגֻלָּה. In keeping with the parallel clause in verse 21 (in Heb.), there should have been a disjunctive accent on עשׂה ; and then we could have read as in the R.V.—"they shall be mine, saith the Lord of hosts, in the day that I do make, even a peculiar treasure". But the accentuator desired to emphasise the personal pronoun—"in the day that *I* do make"—and introduced the dichotomy at this point, even at the risk of confusing the syntax by placing a conjunctive accent on the verb. It is this confusion that is reproduced in the rendering of the A.V., where סגלה is read as accusative after עשׂה—"in that day when I make up my jewels". It is not the jewels however, that are

made up on that day. Even now they are God's
purchased possession, and do not require to wait
for the day of His appearing before they can be
assured of their final destiny. It is the day, and
not the jewels, that is the object of the verb;
and the idea seems to be that whether the faithful remnant be recognised as God's valued pro-
perty here or not, the day approaches, the day
which the Lord has appointed for the Messianic
fulfilment, when they who fear the Lord and
think upon His name shall be acknowledged
before angels and men as His " peculiar treasure."

סגלה, therefore, is not an accusative after עשה,
as the Masoretic accents seem to suggest; but is
to be taken as exegetical of the former part of
the verse, and translated " *und sie sollen mein
Sondereigen werden* ".[1]

The thought that fills the prophet's mind is
the position and prospects of God's faithful
remnant.

(1) Their present standing in grace.

(2) Their future standing in glory.

And the two ideas may well stand side by side
though they are but two aspects of one and the
same divine fact—a covenant relation between

[1] Wellhausen, who gives, however, a slightly different
meaning to אשר אני עשה.

Jehovah and His people which not even death shall be allowed to sever. "Unto you that fear my name shall the sun of righteousness arise with healing in his wings; and ye shall go forth and gambol as calves of the stall."

Another illustration of the more effective pointing of the Masoretes may be found at Isa. i. 21. Common editions, like Theile's, have *Zaqeph* on "judgment": but Baer and Ginsburg appeal to the best codices and editions for *R'bhia*. And rightly so; for the word is subordinate to Tiphcha's clause, not to Silluq's. It ought to read:—

How has become an harlot,
The city that was faithful!
Full of judgment, righteousness used to lodge in her;
But now assassins.

See further, *Sermons in Syntax*, chap. iii.

CHAPTER IV

THE DIFFERENT KINDS AND USES OF THE ACCENTS

THE element of music referred to in the foregoing chapter may help us to explain three other facts connected with the accentual system. (1) The differences between the prose and the poetic accents. (2) The circumstance that the accents in general are used to indicate the tone. (3) The no less significant feature that they consist of two separate classes, distinctives and connectives, or *domini* and *servi,* as the older grammarians used to style them—the former representing the main changes that dominate the verse, and the latter serving or preparing the way for these necessary fluctuations. Before we come to examine the different graphical signs in detail, let us enumerate the salient points connected with these three facts.

1. THE POETICAL ACCENTS

As is well-known the three poetical books— Psalms, Proverbs, and Job—are distinguished by a different accentuation from the twenty-one prose books. In some respects this is a simpler notation than the corresponding prose scheme. It has to do with much shorter *P'suqim* or verses, and therefore does not need to cope with so great a variety of clauses as in the ordinary notation. Yet if it be simpler in interpunction, it is richer in musical effect—having been designed by the Palestinian Rabbis to give a more impressive melody to the chanting of the three books. The Jewish Synagogue, indeed, was not alone in the adoption of such a system. A similar refinement in the cantillation of the Psalms was introduced into the Greek and Latin Churches. So that in view of this development in the liturgical service of the Church, the advent of a poetical accentuation to express the richer flow of the music is not to be regarded as anything anomalous.

Music, not logic, is the key to the different modulation. Logically or syntactically, there was no necessity for its introduction. Books like the Song of Songs or Lamentations, and passages like the Blessing of Moses or the Song of Deborah are just as rich in poetic imagery as any part of the three books : and yet it was not considered necessary to accent these portions of Scripture according to this musical notation. Further, the same passages which are found in one part of Scripture with the poetic accents, are found in other parts with the prose accents —showing that the latter were deemed of sufficient value to give the logical and syntactical relation of the words (*cf.* Psalms xviii., cv. 1-15, with 2 Sam. xxii., 1 Chron. xvi. 8-22). And if additional proof were needed, it is found in the Babylonian system of accentuation, which had no separate notation for the three books at all. For instance, in Job xxxvi. 11, the greatest pause is at "serve him," and this, according to the poetical accentuation, is *Olev'yored ;* but in the superlinear pointing, as in the prose books generally, it is *Athnach*—the principal pausal accent within the verse. These facts seem to suggest that what we have in this system of notation is not a poetic accentuation as such ; but a musical refinement peculiar to the Tiberian school of Masoretes, and specially adapted to the shorter verses of Psalms, Proverbs and Job. Its one idea seems to have been to compensate for the shortness of the verse by a fuller and richer melody in the reading. Hence the conclusion of Dr. Wickes may be accepted as probably correct, that the refinement in question was neither logical nor syntactical, but something of " a purely musical character ".

4

2. THE MARKING OF THE TONE

By tone or accent is meant the stress of the voice which falls generally on the last syllable of the word, as אֶחָד (Gen. i. 5). In certain cases it may fall on the penult, as in the s'golate nouns הָאָרֶץ, הַחֹשֶׁךְ (verses 1, 4), and in certain verbal forms as וַיֹּאמֶר (ver. 3). Indeed, in most instances, a knowledge of the Hebrew grammar is all that is necessary for indicating the position of the tone syllable. For example, we write כִּפַּרְתָּ as 2nd masc. perf., the light termination (*ta*) not being sufficient to bear the weight of the accent; but when we come to the use of vav consecutive with the *perfect*, and learn that it usually throws forward the accent on the ultima, we have to point the word as in Gen. vi. 14, וְכָפַרְתָּ. A similar change, though in quite a different direction, is frequently met with in connection with vav consecutive with the *imperfect*. If circumstances permit it, there is a retrocession of the tone to the penult, so that instead of the usual form of the imperfect יְגָרֵשׁ (Ex. xi. 1), we have the jussive form וַיְגָרֶשׁ with the accent Darga on the open syllable (Deut. xxxiii. 27), *cf.* וַיֹּאמֶר

already referred to. Forms like וַיִּבְרָא וַיִּקְרָא (Gen. i. 8, 21) with accent on the final syllable need occasion no surprise ; for the receding of the tone can only take place when the ultima is originally short, and when the penult which is to receive the tone is an open syllable. Failing these conditions, there is no appreciable change in the jussive form. These and similar details in the marking of the tone may be easily ascertained from a fairly accurate knowledge of grammar and syntax.

But there are other peculiarities connected with the tone-syllable that are not ascertainable in this way. We must have recourse to the laws of Hebrew accentuation. One of these laws is a strong dislike to two accented syllables coming together, unless the former is sufficiently marked by a distinctive accent. Apart from this safeguard the two accents are apt to clash or coalesce, and the full value of their respective melodies to be impaired or lost. Take, *e.g.*, the phrase וְאָכַלְתָּ שָׁם in Deut. xiv. 26. Here we have an instance of vav consecutive with the perfect, and therefore like the examples already given the accent ought to be thrown forward on the ultima (*cf.* וְשָׂמַחְתָּ in the same verse). But since this would bring two accents into juxtaposition, and disturb the delicate harmony of the accentual system, it was allowed to remain on the penult, so as to provide a sufficient hiatus between the two.

The same result was reached in another way. Instead of driving back the tone to the penultima, the accent of the former word was removed altogether by joining the two words by means of *maqqeph*, *cf.* וְהִכְרַתִּי־רֶכֶב (Zech. ix. 10), and וְהִשְׁלַחְתִּי־בָהּ (Ezek. xiv. 13). Another illustration of the same usage is found in phrases like רֹעֵה צֹאן (Gen. iv. 2) that illustrates the former expedient, and עֲצֵי־גֹפֶר (vi. 14), which exemplifies the latter. In both instances the collision of two accented syllables was successfully averted, and a peculiarity of Hebrew prosody explained by the laws of accentuation.

It is but a slight modification of the same rule, when we meet with vav consecutive with the perfect in its *pausal* form. The tone is not thrown forward on the ultima, as in the examples quoted. On the contrary, the word being in pause, the voice seeks a more suitable resting-place on the syllable immediately before the tone, and having lengthened the vowel of this syllable by the weight of its own emphasis, it allows the tone to revert to the penult, as וְשָׂבַעְתָּ (Deut. viii. 10), and וְהָלַכְתִּי (Judg. iv. 8). This usage is fairly uniform with the greater distinctives, *Silluq* and *Athnach* ; but it is also found with Zaqeph, Tiphcha, R'bhia, and Pashta : *cf.* קָרָאוּ and יֵלֵכוּ (Hos. vii. 11, 12). It is even found with D'chi, a comparatively weak accent in the poetical accentuation, as אֶצְדָּק (Job. ix. 20). In this case, the vowel of the accented syllable is not always lengthened as with the greater distinctives. The weaker accents may have the power of retaining the tone on the penult ; but they do not, at the same time, invariably lengthen the vowel on which the tone rests, *cf.* וְאָכַלְתִּי (Deut. ii. 28), and וְעָצַרְתִּי (Isa. lxvi. 9). In fact, the Masoretic instinct which endowed the greater accents with such influence and weight, was not so confident and decided with respect to the minor distinctives. One punctuator boldly retains the tone, and lengthens the vowel, even with so weak an accent as the poetical D'chi : but another hesitates, and does not lengthen the vowel with so strong a pausal accent as Zaqeph. Obviously it is not logic alone that explains so

great a variety in the Masoretic notation. It
is the subtle influence of an underlying melody.
It is logic and melody combined.

3. DISTINCTIVES AND CONNECTIVES

Every Hebrew word, without exception, is
supplied with an accent of some sort, and sometimes with more than one—a fact which shows
how much more elaborate the Hebrew notation
is than our modern system of interpunction. It
is a magnificent effort to reproduce the rhyth-
mical or syntactical relation of each separate
word. And as each word is separated from, or
connected with, the word which immediately
follows, it is marked in every instance by a disjunctive or a conjunctive accent. The larger distinctives indicate the great pauses in the verse,
leaving the finer shades of meaning to be marked
by the minor accents; while the different connectives come in between to prepare the way
for these changes, or help the distinctives, major
or minor, to fill out and regulate the sense. In
short, if the disjunctive accents are the masters
(*domini*) who rule or dominate the verse, the
conjunctives are their loyal servants (*servi*) who
assist them in their multifarious labours.

In Hab. i. 3 we have the somewhat anomalous
form, a double Mer'kha (τ), which is neither dis-

junctive nor conjunctive, or perhaps is a combination of both.

וַיְהִי רִיב וּמָדוֹן יִשָּׂא׃

The R.V. renders, "and there is strife, and
contention riseth up"—two distinct beats in the
music, and two separate steps in the thought.
This however, would require the accent T'bhir on
the second word, as רִיב (Theile), and not simply
the double Mer'kha, as in Ginsburg, Baer and
Wickes. The thought of the Masorete was
deeper. He felt instinctively that the existence
of strife and the rising up of contention were
not two different steps in Israel's sin; but one
and the same picture of violence, which ought to
be joined together, as "spoiling and violence" in
the previous clause. But why then not use the
simple Mer'kha as conjunctive to Tiphcha, and
place a minor distinctive on וַיְהִי ? For the obvious reason that while "strife and contention"
make a common subject to "riseth up," they are
also logically connected with the preceding verb,
and ought to be accented as such. The term
רִיב, in other words, looks both before and after;
and while the disjunctive T'bhir is too strong to
mark it, Mer'kha the conjunctive is too weak.
The accentuator, therefore, introduced the hybrid

accent, a double Mer'kha to accomplish the end
in view : and this, as most authorities agree, is
simply a weakened T'bhir, or T'bhir and Mer'kha
combined. Hence we may render approximately,
" spoiling and violence are before me : and there
is strife and contention that riseth up."   Doubtless the combination of a singular verb with a
double or plural subject is a considerable licence :
but the unity of thought between the two sub-
stantives is a sufficient justification, just as we
read in Jer. vi. 7 : " Violence and spoil is heard
in her "; or in *Paradise Lost* :—

> For the mind and spirit remains
> Invincible.   (Bk. I., 139.)

With respect to the different values of distinctives and connectives, the preacher will find an
instructive illustration at Hab. ii. 4 :—

וְצַדִּיק בֶּאֱמוּנָתוֹ יִחְיֶה :

This is the usual pointing, as in Theile and Baer,
who place a disjunctive accent on *faith* and a
conjunctive on *just*.   And if the accentuator
meant to emphasise " faith " as being in any sense
the principle of life, he had no better means of
accomplishing his object than by putting Tiphcha
on אֱמוּנָה.   But was this the accentuator's meaning ?   Or better still, was this the meaning of

Habakkuk? We scarcely think that it was.
There is no word for "faith" as an active principle of life in the whole Hebrew language;
though the term "believe" is derived from the
same root as the present word.[1] The expression
אֱמוּנָה is not *faith* but *faithfulness*—a term
equivalent to trustworthiness of character or
honesty in conduct; and therefore differing little
from the cognate words integrity and righteousness. *Cf.* the marginal reading of the R.V.
"the just shall live in his faithfulness". Hence
a different accentuation is proposed by Wickes
and Ginsburg— וְצַדִּיק בֶּאֱמוּנָתוֹ יִחְיֶה. In support of this notation we have the rule that when
the subject precedes, it is marked by a disjunctive
accent: and Wickes maintains that he found the
word so accented in the great majority of codices
which he collated. The idea expressed by the
prophet is not the contrast between unbelief and
faith, but that between the fate of the wicked
and the destiny of the just. Amid the storm-
clouds that were gathering around the nation, the
wicked would perish in the flames of his own
kindling; but the just, the faithful remnant,
would not die: they would live in and through
the righteousness they had cultivated as their

[1] A. B. Davidson, *in loco.*

own; and this is the meaning of the emended
accents :—

But the *just*—in his faithfulness shall *live*.

This then is the twofold answer given to the
prophet's prayer. It has laid down a principle
so vital that Habakkuk is told to write it upon
a tablet, and hang it up before the people.

(1) *The fate of the wicked* (first line).

Arrogancy and unrighteousness are the nature
of his sin, and no other doom is needed; these
are the flames in which he and his ill-gotten gains
shall ultimately perish.

(2) *The lot of the righteous* (second line).

After the dark storm-cloud has spent its fury
and rolled away to the horizon, the faithful nu-
cleus of God's Israel shall be left in possession of
a fuller and richer life: and no other reward is
needed; "the just shall *live* in his faithfulness".

On the anacoluthon of a singular verb with a plural subject (p. 56) *cf*. J. H. Moulton's remarks on the "Pindaric"
construction in his Grammar of New Testament Greek, *Pro-
legomena*, p. 58.

CHAPTER V

THE MAIN DISTINCTIVES

THE first step in the accentuation of a piece of composition was the arranging of the text into a number of small divisions called P'suqim or verses (פָּסוּק "cut off"). They are not to be confounded with our logical periods, though it may happen that the Hebrew verses and our English sentences are frequently coterminous. The arrangement is musical rather than logical, and numerous instances occur where the two systems are openly at variance. A passage like Gen. iii. 17-19 contains three distinct P'suqim, but only one logical period; whereas in ch. iv. 7, we have two logical periods in one Hebrew verse. Logically a connection may exist between two or more Hebrew verses, but musically and therefore accentually no such connection exists. Each Pasuq or verse is to be taken and accented independently.

1. SILLUQ (סִלּוּק)

This is the greatest of all the distinctives and is placed under the last word in the verse. The

name signifies " cessation " or " close," and is well
chosen to express the ever-recurring pause in the
melody. Its position below the line may be taken
as a kind of manual sign indicating the close of
the cantillation. The hand of the teacher would
rise and fall with the different accents, like the
conductor's baton in a modern orchestra directing
the rise and flow of the music. Compare the
upraised finger for Zaqeph (ֱ), the meandering
direction of Ṣinnor (ᷰ), the backward inclination
of D'chi (ֽ) and the final pause, if not the sinking
of the hand, in Silluq (ֽ). The manual signs were
thus reproduced, more or less, in the written accentuation. It was photographed phonography.

The present accent is always accompanied by
Soph Pasuq (׃) "verse-end," but is not to be
identified with it. The position of these two dots
at the close of the verse shows that they have
little or nothing to do with our present system
of accentuation. They are a relic of an earlier
and simpler notation in which a single point
marked the division at Athnach, and two the close
of the verse at Silluq. Thus :—

בְּרֵאשִׁית בָּרָא אֱלֹהִים אֵת הַשָּׁמַיִם

וְאֵת הָאָרֶץ ׃

This is the reason why a simple stroke was deemed
sufficient for the final accent. The end of the

verse was marked already by Soph Pasuq. Otherwise the greatest of all the distinctives would
certainly have had a more prominent sign.

With regard to the *servant* of Silluq, there is
considerable diversity between the prosaic and the
poetic books. In the prose accentuation it is
always *Mer'kha* (מֵירְכָא), as, עַל־פְּנֵי הַמָּיִם
(Gen. i. 2). The name is derived from the root
ארך in Hiphil, "to make long"; and therefore denotes an accent that prolongs the modulation.
But in the poetic accentuation Mer'kha is often
replaced by Munach, especially when the tone is
on the first syllable; or when, through the law of
transformation, Silluq is preceded by two or even
by three servi (*cf.* Ps. i. 1, 6). Of course, if Silluq's clause be too short to admit a connective
accent on the preceding word, or if the laws of
accentuation demand a distinctive as a foretone
to Silluq, the prose system introduces Tiphcha as
the musical foretone, and the poetic notation the
corresponding accent R'bhia mugrash, as:—

בֵּין מַיִם לָמָיִם׃ (Gen. i. 6).

הֲפֵצֵי רָעָתִי׃ (Ps. xl. 15).

There is but one connection in which this foretone fails. If a strong logical pause falls on the
first word before Silluq, it may be marked by a

greater distinctive than Tiphcha; and then there is no room for any additional accent between them (Gen. i. 3). The five passages in which the Palestinian authorities have introduced Tiphcha on the same word with Silluq are quite exceptional (*cf.* Hos. xi. 6). It is probably nothing more than a substitute for Metheg.

2. ATHNACH (אֶתְנֶחָ)

The name is derived from a secondary form of נוּחַ, and means "that which causes to rest or pause". In the superlinear punctuation (Cod. Bab.) the form is ⌐; but Wickes is of opinion that originally it was ⌐, a compound sign made up of Silluq and Tiphcha. This would represent Athnach as an intermediate accent, neither so strong as the former, nor so weak as the latter.

Its position in the verse is anything but uniform. In some instances it divides the verse into two fairly equal portions (Gen. i. 8); but at other times the division is so unequal that Athnach may appear on the first word of the verse (xxxiv. 31), or on the first word before Silluq (i. 3). What is the explanation of this variety? The answer is found in various directions; but we may begin with what is known as Hebrew parallelism. *Parallelismus mem-*

brorum is the great formative principle of
Hebrew composition, and is found in its simplest
form in the couplet or distich of the poetical
books.

> A righteous man regardeth the life of his beast :
> But the tender mercies of the wicked are cruel.

Here the two lines balance one another in
thought and in expression, and sometimes no
other guide is needed for a satisfactory rendering of the verse. *Cf.* Job iv. 6. According to
A. B. Davidson's early volume on Job, it would
puzzle Oedipus to drag any meaning from the
rendering of the A.V. But when we note the
principle of parallelism, and the position of
Athnach as marking it, all is plain :—

> Is not thy fear (of God) thy confidence,
> And thy hope the uprightness of thy ways ?

The position of *vav* in the second line is no
doubt peculiar, but not uncommon. Hope is
placed first for the sake of emphasis, and then
what is said of it is introduced by *vav apodoseos*
(*cf.* xix. 23, xxiii. 12, etc.).

The parallelism of members, however, is not
always so simple as this. Indeed such verses
would soon become wearisome by their mono-
tony. The poets, therefore, and much more the
prose writers, allow themselves the utmost

liberty in varying the form of the parallelism. Take, *e.g.*, the triplet or tristich in Hebrew poetry :—

> As the cold of snow in the time of harvest,
> So is a faithful messenger to them that sent him ;
> For he refresheth the soul of his master.

It is not possible to divide this verse into two equal sections. The parallelism is contained in the first two lines, and had these stood alone, the dichotomy would have come between them ; but a third line having been added to explain or qualify the second member, the cæsura was delayed until the main statement of the verse had been set before the hearer. In this way the position of Athnach is determined by the close of the parallelism. In other instances, the arrangement is quite different. The dichotomy is allowed to stand in the middle of the parallelism, and the additional statement prefixed or appended as a subordinate clause :—

> I will be as the dew unto Israel :
> He shall blossom as the lily, |
> And cast forth his roots as Lebanon.
>
> (Hos. xiv. 5.)

But sometimes *parallelismus membrorum* fails altogether as a guide to the division of the verse : and we must have recourse to some other principle of classification. As a rule, the position of the dichotomy will be fixed by the *main logical pause* (*cf.* Gen. i. 7, Isa. i. 3, etc.). However, in a system of public recitation other considerations are allowed to exercise considerable influence, and sometimes for the sake of emphasis or musical equilibrium the logical divisions are ignored (Job x. 8).

> Thine hands have framed me and fashioned me |
> Together round about: yet thou dost destroy me.

The balance of the verse is much better preserved by this arrangement than by placing Athnach on the main pause. Similarly in Ps. ii. 6, parallelism and logic are of no real assistance in fixing the accentuation; but we can gather the words into two groups according to their connection in sense and construction, and the dichotomy will come between them :—

> Yet have I set my King |
> On Zion, my holy hill.

Examples of *emphasis* are found with sufficient frequency. Had these been awanting, indeed, we might well have questioned the taste of the accentuators. But as pointed out in Chap. I. the principle is already recognised in Gen. i. 1 :—

> In the beginning God created |
> The heaven, and the earth.

Cf. also Isa. xxviii. 16: "Therefore thus saith the

Lord God, Behold I lay in Zion for a foundation
a *stone,* | a tried stone, a precious corner stone of
sure foundation : he that believeth shall not make
haste ". The main logical pause is at *sure founda-*
tion ; for here the description of the stone laid
in Zion ends, and the picture of unruffled confidence begins : and but for the principle of emphatic pointing, the leading accent would have
been placed there to mark the dichotomy. But
centuries before the accentuators began their
work the ordinary Jewish interpretation of the
stone had found suitable expression in 1 Peter
ii. 6. It was none other than the long-promised
Messiah. And as this was the thought that filled
the mind of the Masorete, he transferred Athnach
from the chief logical pause, and placed it on the
term *stone* for the sake of emphasis.

As remarked above, however, we are not shut
up, in every case, to adopt the Masoretic accentuation. Each passage must be investigated on
its own merits. Take, *e.g.,* the pointing of Hab.
i. 11 :—

$$\text{אָז חָלַף רוּחַ וַיַּעֲבֹר וְאָשֵׁם זוּ כֹחוֹ}$$
$$\text{לֵאלֹהוּ :}$$

The punctuator has placed the main dichotomy
at אשם, and with the present Masoretic text, it

is hard to see what else he could have done. The
sense of the words, though not the rhythm of the
verse, points to this verb as the only suitable
position for the main logical pause. So that we
may render, " Then he sweeps onwards as a blast,
and passes through and becomes guilty : even he
whose might is his God ". Yet any one can feel
that in this arrangement the balance of the sentence has been sacrificed to the exigencies of the
logic ; and if we add to this the anomalous position
and form of זוּ, which is taken as the demonstra-
tive זֶה in the A.V., but as the relative אֲשֶׁר in
the R.V., we are probably justified in concluding
that the Masoretic text itself is not above suspicion.
Adopting a remark of Graetz, who would compare
this passage with Isa. xl. 31, Wellhausen has suggested the following emendation :—

אז יחלף כוח ואבר וישם

This certainly has the merit of restoring the
rhythm to the verse, and furnishing a natural
and intelligible meaning ; though even he admits
that the difficulties of the text are not yet satis-
factorily surmounted, and that the appearance of
זוּ especially is not easily explained. But assum-
ing some such emendation as the original form of
the text, we might arrange it as follows :—

אָז חָלַף כֹּחַ וַאֲבֹר וַיָּשֶׂם זוּ כֹחוּ
לֵאלֹהוּ :

Then he gains new power and wing,
And makes this his might to be his god.

The *servant* of Athnach is always *Munach*
(מוּנָח). It is also called "Shophar of rest"—
the name referring to the shophar-class ($\overline{}\,\underline{}\,\overline{\,<\,}$),
so named because of their fancied resemblance to
the שׁוֹפָר, "trumpet," used by the Jews on certain
festival days. Like Mer'kha before Silluq, Munach may be replaced by Tiphcha on the first word
before Athnach, if the requirements of the decla-
mation demand a distinctive instead of a connective accent. And as in Silluq's case, so also
in Athnach's, the Palestinian authorities have
specified certain instances in which Tiphcha may
appear on Athnach's word (*cf.* Jer. ii. 31). But
here again the accentuation is quite anomalous;
unless in these cases we can regard Tiphcha as a
servant, or set it on one side as a substitute for
Metheg.

3. S'golta (סְגוֹלְתָּא֘)

It is so named because of its resemblance to
the vowel sign S'gol. Still the *three* points, as
an accentual symbol, have a meaning of their
own. They are to be viewed in relation to the

two points for Zaqeph and the *single* point for
R'bhia. Musically and relatively, S'golta is a
greater pausal accent than Zaqeph, as Zaqeph, in
turn, is greater than R'bhia ; but as the connection between them is musical rather than logical,
they are only found in this relative gradation,
when the length of the verse or the requirements of the melody permit it (Gen. i. 7).

As remarked in Chap. IV. the accents in general
indicate the tone-syllable of the word ; but in
S'golta we have our first illustration of the so-
called *postpositives*. Like Pashta, in the same
verse, it is placed on the last consonant of the
word, because, as suggested by the Grammarians,
its three points in any other position would have
been in danger of colliding with others that
appear above the word, as יְהוֹשֻׁעַ. With the
accent on the penult the postpositives are generally repeated (at least in the Baer and Delitzsch
texts), once on the final consonant as indicating
the regular place of the accent, and once on the
penult to mark the tone syllable (*cf.* הָרְקִיעַ and
הַמַּיִם in the passage quoted). There is but one
slight exception to this rule. In a case like
וַיֹּאמֶר in Gen. xxviii. 13, the repetition of
S'golta would again mix up the points with the

sign of Holem ; and therefore for the sake of clearness it is omitted.

With respect to its pausal value there can be no question that S'golta is a subordinate accent in Athnach's clause. *Cf.* the passage already referred to. " And God made the firmament, ($\stackrel{.}{-}$) and divided the waters which were under the firmament from the waters which were above the firmanent : ($\stackrel{-}{\wedge}$) and it was so." The relative value of these two pauses is suitably expressed in this verse by our comma and colon; and this is the relation, musical and logical, that exists between S'golta and Athnach. Like Zaqeph and R'bhia to be mentioned later, it is essentially subordinate to Athnach.

The preacher will find a good example of these main divisions at Hab. iii. 2 :—

> O Lord, I have heard the report of thee, and am afraid : ($\stackrel{.}{-}$)
> O Lord, revive thy work in the midst of the years,
> In the midst of the years make it known ; ($\stackrel{-}{\wedge}$)
> In wrath remember mercy.

In fixing the position of Athnach in this verse, the first line does not count. The prayer itself is contained in the last three lines, and as the second of the three is merely an expansion of the first, the main dichotomy comes at the close of both to separate the appeal for renewal from the

additional cry for mercy. Hence Athnach is
placed at "known," the greatest logical pause
within the verse. Then the first line of the verse
is prefixed to the prayer proper by means of
S'golta; and as this, in turn, has to be subdivided
into two minor clauses, these are marked by
R'bhia and Zarqa according to the regimen of
S'golta's clause.

The idea expressed by the prophet is the need
of a divine manifestation—a solemn μαρὰν ἀθά.
He has been brooding over the signal tokens of
Jehovah's presence in the past history of his
people—from the day they crossed the Red Sea
to the time they entered, as an armed host, the
land promised to their fathers. And the retro-
spect fills him with awe. "O Lord, I have heard
the report of thee, and am afraid." Yet dreadful
though these past revelations were, the man of
God feels that a similar *Weltkrisis* is needed in the
near future, if ever a new Israel, worthy of that
past history, is to surmount and outlive the dark
days of Jehoiakim. "O Lord, revive thy work
in the midst of the years." In our own age, stir
up Thy ancient might; and even though it be a
dies irae, let the nations know they are but men.
Yea, in the midst of the years make *Thyself*
known. [The LXX reads the reflective form of
the verb, γνωσθήσῃ i.e., תִּוָּדֵעַ the imperf. Niphal,

instead of the Hiphil תּוֹדִיעַ.]　Let the day of the
coming renewal be a Theophany.　But who may
abide the day of His coming ?　With deep insight
and peerless humility he adds, " in wrath remember mercy ".　Amid the darkening storm that is
gathering around the nation, let Thy will be done
and Thy Kingdom come : but O forget not those
who wait for Thee in truth—in wrath remember
mercy.

So that a natural division of the prophet's
prayer would be :—

(1) Its *basis* in the history of the past (S'golta's
clause).

(2) Its *substance*, or a divine manifestation in
the near future (Athnach's clause).

(3) Its *spirit*, as seen in a humble appeal for
mercy on that day, *cf.* 2 Tim. i. 8 (Silluq's clause).
It is Jehovah alone who can give the answer : the
suppliant can only be directed to Him.

> Look not to me—no grace is mine ;
> But I can lift the Mercy-sign.
>   This wouldst thou ? Let it be !
> Kneel down, and take the word divine
>   *Absolvo Te.*[1]

[1] Newman, *Verses on Various Occasions*, p. 83.

CHAPTER VI

THE MINOR DISTINCTIVES

THE whole verse having been divided into sections by the main distinctives, we have next to inquire how these, in turn, were prepared for musical recitation. Each section, supposing it to be of sufficient length, was treated in the same way as the verse itself. It was subdivided into two parts by a minor distinctive, and these again by a still weaker accent, until we arrive at what is termed the *continuous dichotomy*, the most distinguishing feature of Hebrew accentuation (*cf.* the passage cited above) :—

> I will be as the dew unto Israel : (∸)
> He shall blossom as the lily, (⁻ₐ)
> And cast forth his roots as Lebanon.

Here the main dichotomy is fixed, not by the chief logical pause at *Israel*, but by *parallelismus membrorum* at *lily*. For the last two lines both in thought and expression are parallel to one another, and Athnach is placed between them. This leaves the introductory statement, which is ex-

77

planatory of the whole verse, to be prefixed to
Athnach's clause by means of a subordinate accent. In other words, Athnach's clause has been
divided musically into two parts by the minor
distinctive Zaqeph. Finally, each of the three
parts into which the whole verse is now arranged,
may be still further divided into two musical
beats by another disjunctive accent. Hence
Pashta, the foretone to Zaqeph, and Tiphcha,
which performs a similar service to both Athnach and Silluq, are introduced to complete the
accentuation. So that the natural divisions of
our text are :—

(1) The *beauty* and *strength* of the righteous,
as set forth in the members of the parallelism.

(2) The *source* and *secret* of their spiritual ex-
cellencies, expressed in the prefatory clause.

In the present chapter we confine our attention
to the three distinctives—Zaqeph, Tiphcha and
R'bhia.

1. Their Names

(1) *Zaqeph* (זָקֵף). The name is probably to
be explained by the "upright" finger employed
as a manual sign to indicate the character of the
melody (זָקַף "to erect"). The choice of two dots,
instead of an upright line, to represent it has
been alluded to already. It was to denote

its intermediate position between R'bhia and S'golta. But that the upright line was not lost sight of is obvious from the form of double Zaqeph—the so-called *Zaqeph Gadhol*, cf. וְעֵץ (Gen. ii. 9). The difference between these two accents is simply musical, and editors are by no means agreed as to their usage. Sometimes the one sign, sometimes the other is found in the different MSS.; and it seems hardly possible or desirable to draw a distinction between them. Wickes maintains that the latter should only be used when Zaqeph stands entirely alone, with neither servant nor emphasis upon its word (*cf.* Gen. iii. 10). And therefore in a form like וּכְגַנָּה (Isa i. 30), he would introduce this double Zaqeph in place of the ordinary pointing. But Baer and Ginsburg see no such necessity. It is not a difference in pausal value that is claimed for the second accent; consequently no good end is to be served by multiplying the sign.

(2) *Tiphcha* (טִפְחָא). This name means "handbreadth" (from טָפַח in Piel, "to spread out"), and probably refers to the "outspread hand," which would be used as a manual sign in teaching the cantillation. But unfortunately in these matters we can never advance far beyond a

plausible conjecture. Another name, however, given to this accent is the *Tarcha* of the poetic books; and this may help to give tone and character to the melody. It is connected with טָרַח "a burden" (from טָרַח in New Hebrew, "to toil"), and may consequently denote a slow, labouring melody which would be natural enough before the sinking of the voice at Athnach and Silluq. The other name *D'chi*, "thrust back," which is also used in the poetic accentuation, may point to the same general conclusion. It refers to the retarding or thrusting back of the melody before Silluq. Either of these names—the outspread hand in Tiphcha, the labouring melody in Tarcha, or the backward inclination of D'chi, would be a suitable enough designation for this significant foretone. For whether it be found in Athnach's or in Silluq's clause, it always prepares the way for the greater accent.

(3) *R'bhia* (רְבִיעַ). The explanation of this name has been sought in connection with רְבִיעִי, "fourth," as if it referred to its position in the accentual system, the *fourth* after Silluq, Athnach and Zaqeph, or reflected perhaps the additional detail that in its original form the point was not round but four-cornered. It is so printed

throughout Ginsburg's text. But Wickes is convinced that the word R'bhia has nothing to do
with the Ordinal numeral. It is an Aramaic
word, allied to the Hebrew רְבַץ "to lie down"; and
therefore means "resting" or pause. Yet as its
position above the line would seem to indicate a
high note, the resting is to be applied, not to any
sinking of the melody, but to the modulation of
the voice as resting or dwelling on one and the
same note, neither ascending nor descending in
the scale.

2. Their Position

The position of Zaqeph and Tiphcha depends
largely on the length of the verses. In the case
of short P'suqim they may even mark the *main*
dichotomy instead of Athnach (*cf*. Isa. ii. 18, viii.
5; Gen. xxiii. 12). In these passages the greater
distinctive does not appear at all. The rule is
that the nearer the main cæsura approaches to
Silluq, the greater is the tendency to use a minor
distinctive to mark it. The heavier accent was
not considered necessary to conserve the balance
of the modulation. No doubt for the sake of
emphasis or logical interpunction Athnach may
be found even on the first word before Silluq
(Gen. i. 3), and still more on the second, third or
fourth (verses 5, 10, 17); but it is not until we

come to the *fifth* word or *further* that Athnach
is used invariably for the main dichotomy (iii. 5).

A similar confusion or overlapping of accents
is seen in the first half of the verse. In a great
variety of instances the main division in Athnach's
clause may be marked by S'golta or Zaqeph in-
discriminately. The proper place for the former
is at a distance from Athnach, but in certain cases
it appears as early as the fifth or even the fourth
word (Deut. iii. 19). Zaqeph, on the contrary,
prefers to be in the near vicinity of Athnach,
though it also may be found, in occasional instances, as far removed as the eighth or the ninth
(2 Chron. xxxii. 21). This implies that on the
sixth or seventh word before Athnach, these two
accents are about equal in frequency; but above
that limit S'golta preponderates as Zaqeph does
below.

For the position of Zaqeph and Tiphcha in
comparatively short clauses, the student may turn
to Silluq's clause in Gen. iii. 5 :—

וִהְיִיתֶם כֵּאלֹהִים יֹדְעֵי טוֹב וָרָע :

And ye shall be as God, knowing good and evil.

In this verse, Athnach itself is on the fifth
word before Silluq. But this leaves four words
in Silluq's own clause which have still to be de-
fined by the minor distinctives. The greatest of

these is Zaqeph; and as the whole clause,
musically and syntactically, falls into two parts
at *God*, it is rightly placed at this point according to the law of the dichotomy. Then between
Zaqeph and Silluq there is still ample room for
the foretone Tiphcha ; and this appears on the
first or second word according to circumstances.
In the present instance its position is determined
by the grammatical relation of the words.
" Good and evil " are two nouns in the same construction, and joined by *vav*, and are naturally
kept together by a connective accent (*cf.* " dust
and ashes " in Gen. xviii. 27). This leaves but
one word, the participle " knowing," as the
bearer of Tiphcha.

True the principle of emphasis or distinctness
of enunciation may demand a different arrangement of these accents. Even in the case of two
nouns, standing in the same construction, and
joined by *vav*, the dichotomy may be placed
between them, as חֶרֶב לַיהוָה וּלְגִדְעוֹן׃

A sword for the Lord and for Gideon.

(Judg. vii. 20.)

This is the pointing adopted by Wickes in
opposition to Baer and Ginsburg, who point it,
as in the previous example, with a distinctive
accent on " sword". Dr. Wickes is undoubtedly

correct. The contrast is not one between the idea of a sword and the two parties, divine and human, for whom it had been unsheathed. It is a contrast between the parties themselves. The shout of battle combines both heaven and earth, but each in its own order. The sword of *Jehovah !* that, first and chief ; and then, after a swift descent into human relations—the sword also of Gideon.

Under Tiphcha, the foretone to Silluq, the preacher will find an instructive passage at Jer. xxiii. 24, "Do not I fill heaven and earth ? saith the Lord". The thought that occupies the prophet's mind is not that of the material universe, filled by the divine presence, but the divine presence itself, which fills both heaven and earth with its illimitable essence. The main pause, therefore, is not to be placed at "earth," as the English rendering would lead us to infer ; but at the phrase "I fill" (lit. *I am full*) where a continuous participle is luminous with meaning for the Old Testament expositor. What is that meaning ? The answer is partly grammatical, and partly exegetical. If מָלֵא "to be full" is employed of a person whose existence fills everything, the idea of *fulness* becomes associated with that of *filling*,

and is construed with an accusative of that
which is filled. It is not simply "I fill" (which
would be better expressed by the Piel), but "*I
am full*, and therefore *I fill* the heaven and the
earth". [1] "No place can either *in*clude him, or
*ex*clude him," says Matthew Henry : and as the
Qal participle reminds us, He is all this, and
does all this, continuously. In fine, syntax and
melody have combined to illumine the entire
paragraph. There is (1) a fulness of *grace ;* for
the God of Israel is not simply a God at hand,
as the false prophets testified, but a God also
afar off (ver. 23)—even among the Babylonians.
(2) A fulness of *judgment*, or the former process reversed. It might fall upon the heathen
at the outermost sweep of the circle; but it
would not rest there. It would move inwards
towards the centre, until, like a "whirling
tempest," the anger of the Lord would sweep
around the walls of Jerusalem (verses 17-20).
(3) A fulness of *promise*, as to the wondrous
power of the prophetic word, when instead of
being prostituted in the hands of the false
teachers (verse 22), it is proclaimed and laid to
heart by the prophets and people of Jehovah.
It is a message which achieves wonders (verses

[1] *Cf.* Ewald's *Lehrbuch*, 281, b.

28, 29). It comes first as the *wheat*; and if only
Israel would receive it as such, it would come
with all the promise and potency of life. But in
proportion as this is rejected, it is transformed
into the similitude of *fire*, which burns and re-
fines, until the alloy, in God's people, is finally
separated from the gold. If this also is re-
sented, and Israel, instead of being softened
like the wax, becomes hardened like the clay,
then the concluding stage in the divine discipline
is reached, when the word of God becomes a
hammer to break the rocks in pieces. And yet
it need not be. It is a fulness of grace, before it
becomes a fulness of judgment. It is a promise
of life before it becomes a visitation of death—a
life that is meant to effloresce in disposition and
character, and bear fruit in an ever-advancing
career of practical beneficence. Wheat, fire,
hammer!—other books may seek our attention,
but this book demands it—

> O my soul, thou hungry bird
> Taste the honey of the word.

3. The Repetition of Zaqeph and R'bhia in Longer Clauses

What changes, if any, are introduced to meet
the exigencies of longer clauses? The first few
words are marked off by Zaqeph and Tiphcha

as already indicated, and then the rest of the
clause is separated into smaller divisions according to the sense or grammatical construction ; and these are denoted by a repetition of
Zaqeph and R'bhia as often as the necessities
of the case permit. *Cf.* Gen. iii. 1, where
Zaqeph occurs no fewer than three times in
Silluq's clause, and twice in Athnach's ; or
xlvii. 6, in which we have a good illustration of
the musical subordination of R'bhia to Zaqeph.
The rule is that if Zaqeph's own clause has a
fairly strong accent on the *second* word, it may
be marked by R'bhia, instead of the foretone
Pashta, and then the musical foretone, being no
longer required on the second word before Zaqeph,
is introduced on the first, and we have the
secution of three distinctives and no servant at
all. The same rule applies, if the pause in question fall on the third word before Zaqeph (Gen.
i. 2). It is frequently marked by R'bhia ; until
beyond that limit, when occurring on the *fourth*
or *further*, it is indicated by R'bhia alone (i. 11).

In illustration of these rules an interesting
example is found at Isa. lxiii. 19 :—

הָיִינוּ מֵעוֹלָם לֹא־מָשַׁלְתָּ בָּם

According to the Masoretic accents the first word
is not to be taken as a separate clause and

rendered as in the A.V. : "We are thine : thou
never barest rule over them ". It is subordinated
to Zaqeph's clause by the ordinary pointing
R'bhia, and is rather to be translated as in the
R.V. : " We are become as they over whom thou
never barest rule ". It is doubtful, however, if
even this rendering has done justice to the Masoretic notation. The first word *is* subordinated to
Zaqeph's clause, but it is subordinated by means
of a disjunctive accent, and this fact may well
be reflected in the translation. The idea the
prophet wishes to express is the contrast between
the holy people who had God for their father
(verse 16), and the adversaries who had come
and trodden His sanctuary under foot (verse 18).
That contrast, alas, seemed to exist no longer.
" We are become—" but how shall he utter the
words ! how shall he bring himself to admit that
Israel, the chosen nation, had become as the un-
circumcised heathen ! He cannot. The disjunctive accent has left a solemn hiatus that
must be filled up in some way, when we try to
represent it in cold print. But in the prophet's
soul it was filled up by no words. It was left to
a silence too deep for speech—a flood of emotion
too deep for tears. " We are become—thou
never barest rule over them ; they were not
called by thy name."

An equally instructive passage may be found
at Jer. xiii. 27. Instead of confining the interrogative part of the sentence to the last two words,
where it is suitably introduced by the particle
מָתַי, the A.V. has carried it back to Zaqeph's
clause and translated it, "Woe unto thee,
O Jerusalem! Wilt thou not be made
clean? when shall it once be?" In view of the
context, however, this is not in any sense an exact
reproduction of the prophet's thought. Under
the figure of every bottle being filled with wine,
Jeremiah has foretold the madness that would
drive the people to destruction (verses 12-14).
No doubt a call to repentance has been added
(verse 16)—an earnest appeal to give glory to
the Lord their God before it is too late, and
their feet stumble on the hills of twilight. But
can the Ethiopian change his skin or the leopard
his spots? Alas, for the answer. The conviction is sorrowfully expressed that all remedies
are hopeless, *because* (LXX, ὅτι) Jerusalem *would
not* be clean. She could not, because she would
not; and therefore the R.V. renders—" Woe unto
thee, O Jerusalem! thou wilt not be made clean:
how long shall it yet be?" A stage comes in
the history of nations, no less than in the experience of individual men, when the preaching of

repentance is not sufficient; when it ought to be supplemented by the solemn reminder that continued refusal to obey may end in something far more solemn—the inability to give obedience; that the *will not* may become the *can not*, and that in such a crisis there is nothing left to the disobedient but the dreaded discipline of exile. "How often would I have gathered thy children together . . . and ye *would not!* Behold, *your house is left unto you desolate*" (Matt. xxiii. 37, 38).

Under R'bhia's clause we have another interesting example at Amos v. 15. "Hate the evil and love the good, and establish judgment in the gate: *peradventure* Jehovah, the God of hosts, may be gracious unto the remnant of Joseph."

For the distinction between the particle אוּלַי and the telic ὅπως of the LXX, see *Sermons in Syntax*, Chap III. It suggests a threefold division :—

1. A call to repentance. (Whole verse.)
2. The human fruits meet for repentance, *viz.*, private rectitude and civic justice. (First half.)
3. The assurance of forgiveness—a forgiveness, however, which must be consistent with divine righteousness. In view of this requirement, the utmost that the prophet will allow himself to affirm is the "peradventure" of a profound humility.

CHAPTER VII

DISTINCTIVES OF LESS DEGREE

In addition to the subordinate accents in Isa. liii. 4, we have an emphatic arrangement of the words which is quite inadequately expressed by the R.V. The first two clauses ought to read :—

> Surely *our* griefs He bore
> And it was *our* sorrows that He carried

—an order that brings out the antithesis so sharply depicted in the sequel :—

> Yet *we* did esteem him stricken,
> Smitten of God, and afflicted.

The first couplet indicates the poignant sorrow of the Lord's Suffering Servant: the second, the false conception entertained by men of His unparalleled woes. Hence the main cæsura is rightly placed at "carried," for here the verse falls into the two halves of an antithetical parallelism. Each half, in turn, is similarly dealt with. The first consists of two members which balance one another in thought and in expression ;

93

and is therefore divided into two parts at "bore" by the minor distinctive Zaqeph. The parallelism of the second couplet is not so easily indicated. In the placing of the disjunctive accent, the accentuator seems to have wavered between the principle of musical equilibrium and the desire to do justice to the vivid contrast between the men who had so ignorantly passed judgment and the One whom they had so seriously misjudged. Had he allowed the former principle to prevail, he might have written as above:—

> Yet we did esteem him stricken, |
> Smitten of God, and afflicted.

This would have been a good example of *partial* parallelism, in which the main idea of the clause is given first, and then follows an echo (as it were) of the last part of it. But in this case the logical contrast would have been sacrified to the balance of the melody. And therefore instead of yielding to this temptation, he places the accent Zaqeph after *him,* and allows the whole description of the suffering servant to be brought under the regimen of Silluq's clause. Thus:—

וַאֲנַ֣חְנוּ חֲשַׁבְנֻ֔הוּ
נָג֕וּעַ מֻכֵּ֥ה אֱלֹהִ֖ים וּמְעֻנֶּֽה׃

This means that not only is Tiphcha introduced as musical foretone to Silluq: but in Tiphcha's own clause there must be a further subdivision at "stricken" by the insertion of the musical forebeat T'bhir. In fine, the continuous dichotomy is only brought to a close, when the length of the clause or the possibilities of the modulation are exhausted.

In the present chapter we confine our attention to the three subordinate accents—Pashta, T'bhir and Zarqa.

1. PASHTA (פַּשְׁטָא)

The name signifies "extending" (from פָּשַׁט "to stretch out"), and is best explained as referring to the melody. It was made *postpositive* to distinguish it from the conjunctive Azla, having the same sign, as וַיִּקְרָא ... לָאוֹר (Gen. i. 5). When Pashta would come on a monosyllabic word or on a dissyllable accented on the penult, and no servant precedes, it is changed into *Y'thibh*—a fine musical distinction, though there is no difference between them in disjunctive value, as in Gen. iii. 1, אַף כִּי־אָמַר אֱלֹהִים. Y'thibh is simply a substitute for Pashta, and is to have the full pausal value of Zaqeph's foretone. The new accent itself was made *pre-*

positive to distinguish it from M'huppakh, the
servant of Pashta, as אֵלֶּה and אֵלֶּה.

With but one *servant* before Pashta, the accent
chosen is generally M'huppakh, except in a few
instances where no syllable intervenes between
the servus and the tone-syllable of Pashta's
word. In this case the conjunctive used is
Mer'kha as הָיְתָה תֹהוּ (Gen. i. 2). But the
question of Pashta's servants is much more
complicated than this. There may be two, three,
four or even five servi with this disjunctive
accent (1 Sam. vii. 10), and as a rule they come
in this order—M'huppakh on the first word
before Pashta, Azla on the second, Little T'lisha
on the third, and beyond that Munachs.
M'huppakh itself is so named from its form,
being an "inverted" Shophar (from הָפַךְ "to
turn"). See *Munach*, Chap. V.

With respect to the position of Pashta in the
accentuation of the clause, the usage is uniform
and not difficult to follow. It is usually found
on the second word before Zaqeph, though it
may also appear on the first or the third (*cf.*
Gen. iv. 7). "If thou doest well, shalt thou not
be accepted? and *if* (וְאִם) thou doest not well,
sin coucheth at the door." The second "if,"

though an unimportant word, has the pausal
accent to indicate emphasis. It is a solemn
alternative that is here placed before the elder
brother, and the decision in either case is his
own. Man is endowed with the terrible power
of saying " no " even to his Maker ; and which-
ever answer he gives he alone will be held
responsible. *"If"*—the very word is like a
rapier thrust into the conscience—" If thou doest
not well, sin coucheth at the door." No more
daring figure was ever uttered. Sin, like a
monster, is ready to spring upon him, and bury
its fangs in his life.

Or see another illustration at ver. 15. "And
the Lord said unto him, *Therefore* (לָכֵן) whosoever slayeth Cain, vengeance shall be taken on
him sevenfold." This verse is specially interesting from the standpoint of the LXX. Instead of
" therefore," it has read " not so " (οὐχ οὕτως, *i.e.*,
לֹא כֵן). And if we bear in mind these two facts,
(*a*) that in the original text the words were not
strictly kept asunder, and (*β*) that the presence
or absence of the quiescent *Aleph* was left in
large measure to the discretion of the scribes, we
can easily understand how the primitive consonants לכן might give rise to both readings. A
parallel illustration is found at 2 Kings vii. 17,

where instead of הַמֶּלֶךְ, "the King," the LXX
must have read המלך, the shortened form of
הַמַּלְאָךְ, "the messenger" (τὸν ἄγγελον). The
rendering of the LXX, in the present instance, is
certainly supported by the context. Cain com-
plains that as a fugitive in the earth his life
would be in constant jeopardy — "whosoever
findeth me shall slay me". But God answers,
"*Not so* (disjunctive accent) whosoever slayeth
Cain, vengeance shall be taken on him sevenfold".
Even at this early stage in the history, a seed-
thought is sown, of which the subsequent growth
will point in a very different direction from the
interminable blood-revenge that dominated primitive society. The city of refuge was already
here in germ—if not the far-off echo of redemp-
tion. And who shall say that the thought as thus
expressed is not worthily represented in the
Masoretic accentuation?

2. T'BHIR (תְּבִיר)

The position of T'bhir, as foretone to Tiphcha,
explains the peculiar form of its graphical sign.
It is an intermediate accent between R'bhia and
Mer'kha—neither so strong as the former nor so
weak as the latter—and therefore appropriately
made up of the forms of both accents (Gen. i. 28).

For the same reason it has the name a *fracture* or break (= Hebrew שֶׁבֶר). It indicates a brief pause in Tiphcha's clause, whether a broken note in the melody or a slight break in the sense. With regard to the servant or servants, the same rules apply as with Pashta. Its own connective is *Darga* (ָ)—a name which seems to denote "a scale or trill," from the Arabic root, "a stair"; but this is frequently replaced by Mer'kha, especially in those instances where, as in Pashta's clause, there is not a sufficient hiatus between the servant and the tone-syllable of T'bhir's word (Gen. i. 26). The other servi are Azla, Little T'lisha and Munach, as in the cases already considered (Amos ix. 7).

A practical illustration that may be brought under this distinctive is found at Isa. xxviii. 28 :—

לֶחֶם יוּדָק כִּי לֹא לָנֶצַח אָדוֹשׁ יְדוּשֶׁנּוּ

The R.V. gives us a choice of readings—introducing a positive statement in the text, and inserting a pointed question in the margin; but we are convinced that both context and accents are in favour of the latter. " Is bread (corn) *crushed?* (Hophal of דָּקַק " to beat in pieces or pulverise," like the calf which Moses reduced to powder in Ex. xxxii. 20, or the Ashera which

Josiah stamped into fine dust in 2 Kings xxiii.
6.) *Nay* (disjunctive accent) he will not ever be
threshing it." The threshing instrument has been
introduced for a purpose; and the moment this
purpose is served, it will be removed instantly.
Is this not the teaching of the context? "Doth
the plowman plow continually to sow?" (ver. 24).
In other words, does the farmer look no further
than the sowing as he steps along the furrows?
Not so; in his own way he is a man of vision.
He sees the end from the beginning. And every
clod he breaks, and every weed he kills, is all
done for a purpose. He lives and plans for the
time when the outcome of his labours shall be set
before his face as bread. And shall He who
taught the husbandman wisdom be found working on a lower level Himself? Surely the parable
of the threshing instrument might teach a different lesson. The hosts of Assyria would not be
allowed to stamp through the land, like some
blind, irresponsible force, and bruise or crush the
good grain along with the chaff. The divine
husbandman knew better. He was working for
a purpose; and the moment this purpose was
achieved, the threshing instrument would be
withdrawn. Is bread corn crushed? Is the process of threshing continued so long that the grain
is not only separated from the chaff, but actually

bruised and destroyed under the threshing instrument? Nay, the husbandman knows when
to stop. He will *not* ever be threshing it. In
Amos's fine language, He may shake Israel among
the nations, like as corn is sifted in a sieve, but
not one good grain shall be permitted to fall upon
the ground. After the threshing instrument and
the winnowing sieve have both done their work,
there will remain His faithful remnant—a golden
heap of good grain piled up on His threshing-floor.

For this use of כִּי to express the negative
answer to a question, see Job xxii. 2:—

> Can a man be profitable unto God?
> *Nay*, he that is wise is profitable unto himself.

3. ZARQA (זַרְקָא֮)

There is little to add respecting this accent
after what has been said of Pashta and T'bhir.
It occupies the same position in S'golta's clause
as these do in Zaqeph's and Tiphcha's. It is
found on the first, second or third word before
S'golta, according to the rules already enun-
ciated; and it is preceded by as many as four
servi (Deut. ix. 4) or by other distinctives like
R'bhia and Pashta (2 Sam. iii. 8) in a way pre-
cisely similar to these two other accents. *Cf.*
Gen. xxviii. 13:—

וְהִנֵּה יְהוָֹה נִצָּב עָלָיו וַיֹּאמַר

" And, behold, the Lord stood above it (or, *beside him*), and said, I am the Lord, the God of Abraham thy father, and the God of Isaac: the land whereon thou liest, to thee will I give it, and to thy seed." The main dichotomy is placed at *Isaac*; for in the accentuation of this verse, the speech itself, and not the words which introduce it, are considered of prime importance, and this is divided into two parts by the distinctive Athnach, as if the introductory words were non-existent. The whole verse as thus arranged is full of interest to the preacher. It sets before us a natural threefold division of the subject:—

(1) *The divine manifestation*—in the prefatory statement.

(2) *The divine faithfulness*—in Athnach's clause.

(3) *The divine promise*—in Silluq's.

But what is the full force of the distinctive Zarqa on the first word before S'golta? Does the preposition with the suffix refer to the ladder or the dreamer? Perhaps in the light of xviii. 8 where Abraham stood *by* (עַל) the three men under the tree, we may be warranted in adopting the latter. Not only did the angels of God

ascend and descend on the mystic stair; but
El-Shaddai, the God of his fathers, had come to
touch the earth, and to make the place and hour
a Bethel. So that when he awoke from his
sleep, it was not to lift his eyes to the heavens
above him, but to glance around in the uncertain
light of dawn, and say, "Surely the Lord is in
this place : and I knew it not" (xxviii., 16).

The name *Zarqa* is interpreted in various
ways. According to Jewish writers it is to be
connected with זָרַק "to scatter," and may have
been applied to a meandering or varying note,
rising and falling about the same pitch or key,
like the technical phrase "a turn" in modern
music. Its designation in the poetic accentuation is *Sinnor* "a pipe or spout"; and certainly its
form suggests a crooked pipe : while in the same
connection, it was made postpositive, as in the
poetic notation, to distinguish it from the conjunctive Sinnorith which has the same form.

In Ex. xx. 8, 9—at least in one of its notations, for as is well known the Decalogue, both
in Ex. xx. and in Deut. v., is dignified by a
double accentuation—we have another illustration of the practical value of this accent. "Remember the Sabbath day, to keep it holy. Six
days shalt thou labour (תַּעֲבֹד) and do all thy

work." The duty of Sabbath *rest* has frequently been emphasised in the exposition of this commandment; but not always with the response or result desiderated by the preacher. Perhaps the time has come to insist on another aspect of this subject—not the rest that ought to characterise the seventh day, but the labour that ought to occupy and fill up the hours of the other six. The truth is, that there are too many idling away the working days in indolence and selfish pleasure to enjoy the rest of the Sabbath, when it falls like a benediction upon the world. And therefore we are to insist with all the variation of thought and figure, so well symbolised by the form of this suggestive accent, that it is honest work no less than Sabbath rest that is the paramount obligation of each human life; and that only those who labour at some worthy God-honouring task, will ever really know what Sabbath rest means. "Six days shalt thou *labour*, and do all thy work: but the seventh day is the Sabbath of the Lord thy God."

CHAPTER VIII

THE LEAST DISTINCTIVES

WITH these accents we come to the last musical and interpunctional divisions, and the principle of the dichotomy which has played so important a part in the subdivision of the verse is now brought to a close. A trace of it may be still found in a few cases under Geresh, where both Pazer and Great T'lisha are utilised as dividers of its clause (Gen. xxvii. 36). But the tendency is to use connectives instead of distinctives at the beginning of the verse; and these are repeated as often as may be required, even though it requires as many as five servi to complete the accentuation (Jud. xi. 17).

1. THEIR NAMES

(1) *Geresh* (גֶּרֶשׁ). The name signifies *extrusion* or *expulsion* (from גָּרַשׁ " to drive out ") and is no doubt to be referred to the strong expulsion of the voice required to produce the melody.

107

It was one of the high notes, placed near the
beginning of the verse to lead off the cantillation; and was naturally pitched on an elevated key to give volume and carrying effect to
the music. The fact that it was weak in pausal
value does not mean that it was weak also in
pitch or musical elevation. The reverse is the
truth. The accents that were feeblest as marks
of interpunction might be strongest and loudest
in their capacity as musical notes.

Another form of the accent is the so-called
double Geresh or *Gersháyim*—a form which,
while it indicates no difference in disjunctive
value, was doubtless introduced to express a
fuller intonation than the single graphical sign.
The divergence in their usage is not difficult to
follow. Simple Geresh may be preceded by no
fewer than five servi—Azla on the first, Little
T'lisha on the second, and the rest Munachs (1
Kings xxi. 2); but double Geresh can never have
more than one, and this always Munach, as
עֵץ פְּרִי (Gen. i. 11).   There is but one connection
in which the same servant may appear on the
first word before simple Geresh. If the whole
clause consists of only two words, and the one
servus that is required fall on the *first letter* of
the word, it is marked by Munach instead of Azla,

as Isa. lx. 17. In all other cases it is *Azla* (אַזְלָא)
a term which seems to denote the simple idea of
"going on," *i.e.*, conjunctive, or not pausing in
the melody (fr. אָזַל "to go"), and therefore well
fitted to distinguish it from the disjunctive
Pashta which has the same sign.

(2) PAZER (פָּזֵר). This accent, as already
pointed out, may mark a further division in
Geresh's clause : and this may help to explain
the form of its graphical sign. It is simply the
sign of Geresh with a pausal stroke added which,
through a slight rounding of the angle, becomes
the Pazer of our texts. The name is derived
from the modulation, which must have been of
the same high character as Geresh. Ben-Asher,
for instance, called it נֵצַח, "conspicuous" or
"clear," in reference, no doubt, to its sharply de-
fined tone. But the verb פָּזַר "to scatter," would
seem to suggest a "shake" or "trill" as the
quality of the note in question, though, even in
this case, it would still be pitched on the same
high level as Geresh. A second form of the
accent is also to be noted. It is known as Great
Pazer, or *Qarne-Pharah*—a name derived from
the twofold figure of its graphical sign, which
some accentuator fancied was not unlike "the

horns of a cow" (קַרְנֵי פָרָה), as הָעִיר (Ezek.
xlviii. 21). The original symbol, however, was
probably ⌣; two fingers turned upward—a
most suitable manual sign for the teaching of the
cantillation. By and by the punctuators began
to amuse themselves with designing ornamental
forms for the various accents, and introduced
the misleading and regrettable form portrayed
above—representing Great Pazer as if it were a
union of the T'lishas. It is needless to say that
no such union exists.

Unlike Little Pazer, the greater accent can
never stand alone. It must always be preceded
by at least two servi, the first of which will be
Galgal, and the rest Munachs. Still the real distinction between the two accents, whether
musical or otherwise, can no longer be appreciated
by us. Little Pazer might easily have stood in
all the sixteen passages where Qarne-Pharah is
now introduced. But here, as at many other
points in the accentual system, we are not in a
position to unravel the secret. The subtilties of
the Masoretes are beyond us.

(3) GREAT T'LISHA—(תְּלִישָׁא)—a *pre*positive
accent, and therefore to be distinguished from
Little T'lisha, a *post*positive. The latter, indeed,
has been so greatly reduced in pausal value that

it has entered the conjunctive class altogether,
although, to begin with, the two signs were
probably nothing more than two forms of one
and the same accent. For this reason they constantly interchange in the different codices and
editions, as וַיִּשְׁלַח (Ginsburg), וַיִּשְׁלַח (Baer) in
2 Sam. v. 11. According to the Grammarians
the original sign was properly a small circle, and
this may be the reason why it was placed at the
beginning or end of the word. It was to avoid
confusion with the circular ᵒ which is used to
call attention to a Masoretic note.

The name T'lisha has been referred by some to
the figure of a shield to which it bears some dis-
tant resemblance. Wickes however regards it as
a musical term (from the root תלש "to pluck out,
or draw out with effort"), indicating that this
accent "drew out" the voice with a marked
effort or impulse. Hence it is rightly classed
with the high notes Geresh and Pazer, as introducing or leading off the melody. The servi of
Great T'lisha, which may number from one to
five, are all Munachs (Jer. xiv. 1).

To mention only one additional point in connection with these accents, we have in Zeph. ii.
15, a choice of two distinctives on one and the
same word. "This (זֹאת) is the joyous city that

dwelt carelessly." A comparison of Gen. i. 9,
with Deut. vi. 5, shows that a minor dichotomy
on the second word before Pashta is sometimes
marked by Geresh, sometimes by Great T'lisha.
And yet in five passages, of which the present is
one, the two accents are found together—an inti-
mation that ancient authorities differed as to the
chanting. The later Masoretes unable to decide
which was right directed that *both* accents
should be written and chanted; and thus we
have the peculiar double form of our present
text.

2. Their Position

They are brought in to mark the accentual
divisions in four different clauses, of which
R'bhia's clause may be taken as the type.
Thus :—

$$\overset{\cdot}{\underset{\text{\tiny $\lrcorner$}}{}} \mid \overset{\prime}{\underset{\text{\tiny $\lrcorner$}}{}} \mid \overset{\circ}{\underset{\text{\tiny $\lrcorner$}}{}} \underset{\text{\tiny $\lrcorner$}}{} \underset{\text{\tiny $\lrcorner$}}{} \text{ etc.} \mid \overset{\nu}{\underset{\text{\tiny $\lrcorner$}}{}} \underset{\text{\tiny $\lrcorner$}}{} \text{ etc.} \mid \overset{\nu}{\underset{\text{\tiny $\lrcorner$}}{}} \text{ etc.}$$

With *two* words in R'bhia's clause (and no more)
the first is usually marked by Munach, but in a
few cases the distinctive Gersháyim is employed,
especially if the words be long (*cf.* Ezek. xiii. 21).
When the clause consists of *three* words (and no
more) the usage varies. A minor pause may
come on the first or second word before R'bhia,
and is marked in either case by Geresh (Gen. i. 28,

Ex. xxxvi. 9). Yet since it was not always considered necessary to emphasise the dichotomy in so short a clause, the lighter melody of a servus is frequently found in the first instance, and a servus with Paseq in the second (Gen. iv. 15, Ex. xxvi. 2). If there be more than three words in R'bhia's clause, the variety in the usage is increased. The main pause may now fall on the third, fourth or fifth word before R'bhia, or even beyond that limit, and the various parts of the extended sentence are arranged and accented accordingly. With the dichotomy on the *third* word before R'bhia the melody divides the honour between Geresh and Great T'lisha. With this difference, however, that if the former be employed to mark the main dichotomy, it must be content with a Paseq to indicate a minor pause on the first or second word; whereas if the main pause is denoted by Great T'lisha, the lighter division may enjoy the advantage of being more adequately represented by Geresh (*cf.* Gen. i. 29, Isa. vii. 4).

A somewhat similar variation occurs with the main pause on the *fourth* word before R'bhia. It may be expressed by any one of the three accents Geresh, Great T'lisha or Pazer. Yet with this difference again that if Geresh be used to mark it, there is no other suitable distinctive

between Geresh and R'bhia than a light Paseq :
whereas Great T'lisha or Pazer would have the
additional advantage of being followed by Geresh
itself (*cf.* Jon. i. 3, 2 Sam. xv. 6, Gen. xxvii. 36).
Finally, when we come to the *fifth* word before
R'bhia, or further, the usage becomes fairly uniform.   There are a few cases where Geresh
appears on the fifth word, and Great T'lisha is
placed even on the sixth, but the regular dividing accent is now Pazer—an accent which may
be repeated more than once according to the requirements of the dichotomy (2 Sam. iii. 21).

That the same rules are applicable to the
clauses governed by Pashta, T'bhir and Zarqa
may be illustrated by Jer. xvii. 20, Isa. lxvi. 19,
Jer. xlix. 19, and Bible *passim*.   In one particular only is there a slight variation.   When a
minor pause is due on the *first* word before
R'bhia, it is marked by Geresh as in the examples
quoted ; but this is not the case with the three
lighter accents Pashta, T'bhir and Zarqa.   As a
rule, transformation takes place.   Geresh is
changed into the appropriate servus before these
three accents ; and the rhythmical cadence at the
close of the clause is purposely omitted (*cf.* Gen.
xliii. 3, 2 Kings xxv. 21, Deut. xxx. 19).   Still in
all such cases of transformation the servi of
Geresh remain, as if the accent in disappearing

from the written page had left its influence
behind it.   Thus :—

וַיֵּדַ֓ אֹתָ֛ם מֶ֥לֶךְ בָּבֶ֖ל וַיְמִיתֵֽם׃

3. Three Special Texts for the Preacher

A good example of Pazer as a minor dichotomy
in Geresh's clause is found at Mal. i. 6 : "A son
honoureth his father, and a servant his master :
if I then be a father, where is my honour ? and
if I be a master, where is my fear ? "   The main
logical pause is placed at *master* ; for here the
picture of filial reverence ends, and the solemn
arraignment of Israel for irreverence begins.
The weight of the logic, if not the balance of the
melody, points to this as the only right position
for Athnach.   Then in Silluq's clause the principle of the dichotomy is continued.   "If I be
a father, where is my honour ? (*Pazer*) and
if I be a master, where is my fear ? (*Geresh*)
saith the Lord of hosts (*R'bhia*) unto you, O
priests, that despise my name. (*Zaqeph*).   And
ye say, Wherein have we despised thy name."
Beginning at the close of the verse and working
backwards, the first important pause is at "my
name"; for at this point the earnest appeal of
Jehovah passes into the unbelieving rejoinder
of the priests.   This, therefore, is marked by

Zaqeph. Then as the next considerable division is on the fourth word before Zaqeph, it is rightly represented by R'bhia, in accordance with the rules of Zaqeph's clause. This leaves two other distinct beats between R'bhia and the beginning of the section, and these are marked by Geresh and Pazer according to the regimen of these accents. Finally, within these main divisions, and as helping to give tone and colour to the general outline, there are various minor details full of interest to the expositor (*cf.* the emphatic contrast between the *saying* of Jehovah and the *saying* of the priests, as reflected in the *Paseq* associated with אמר and the *Zaqeph Gadhol* with אמרתם; and especially the unenviable notoriety given to the priests by the emphatic repetition of Pashta, לָכֶם הַכֹּהֲנִים). The rebuke falls chiefly upon the priesthood, because instead of being penetrated with the holiest reverence for God, these ministers of the altar were mainly responsible for the disregard of Jehovah which had led to the decline of public worship. The whole verse is thus an earnest appeal for *reverence in religion*, and these are its natural divisions.

(*a*) The beauty of reverence, as seen in the illustrations of son and servant.

(β) The lack of this in Israel, who was both Jehovah's son and servant (Hos. xi. 1, Isa. xli. 8).

(γ) The cause of this declension traced to the priests, who were ready to ask in the insensibility of unbelief, "Wherein have we despised thy name?" The pulpit and the pew stand or fall together. "Like people, like priest" has, as its counterpart, "Like priest, like people".

Zeph. iii. 17 is an illustration of R'bhia's clause, where it consists of these words and nothing more. In other respects the passage is interesting both in accents and grammar. In the A.V. it is rendered thus: "The Lord thy God in the midst of thee is mighty; he will save, he will rejoice over thee with joy, etc." This is in no sense an adequate rendering of the Hebrew accents. The main pause is not at "mighty," but at "save;" and therefore we must read as in the R.V. "The Lord thy God is in the midst of thee, a mighty one who will save, etc." It is doubtful, however, if even this translation gives the exact thought of the prophet. The term "save" is a frequentative imperfect, which is often used to form adjectival clauses descriptive of the subject of the preceding sentence, as in Hos. iv. 14, where we read of a people that doth not understand, *i.e.*, an *undiscerning* people; or in Isa. li. 12, where "man that shall die" = *mortal* man. So here: the

idea is not that at some future time the Holy
One of Israel will deliver them from all their
fears; but that in all circumstances they possess
an ever-present salvation, a mighty one who is
strong enough to fortify against all evil—*ein
sieghafter Held* (Wellhausen).

Then in the second half of the verse we have
three clauses governed by Silluq, Zaqeph and
R'bhia, which, like three soundings of the un-
fathomed love of God, tell us something of the
depth and fulness of this covenant relationship.
" He will rejoice over thee with joy, he will be silent
in his love, he will joy over thee with singing."
Israel was something more than Jehovah's son or
servant (Mal. i. 6): she was Jehovah's spouse—
especially in Hosea; and therefore like the lover
who allows himself to be absorbed with quiet joy
in the object of his affection, God's love for Israel
is represented as too deep for speech—it is hushed
into a silent ecstasy. He will rejoice *over thee*.
Will not the converse be equally true that Israel
will rejoice over Him?   His love is infinite, both
in its height and depth.

(*a*) *Its height*; for He has drawn Israel to His
side, that He may shelter and succour her by His
" mighty " arm.

(*β*) *Its depth*; or the deep, silent fervour of
that divine affection which seeks only to have

Israel near, that she may feel the throbbing of its heart. Will not the answer of Israel be?—

> Thou hidden Love of God, whose height,
> Whose depth unfathomed, no man knows,
> I see from far Thy beauteous light,
> Inly I sigh for Thy repose:
> My heart is pained, nor can it be
> At rest till it finds rest in thee.

Finally, in connection with the two T'lishas, we have a choice of readings in 1 Sam. ii. 24. Common editions, like Theile's, have the conjunctive accent (כִּֽי), whereas Baer and Ginsburg prefer the disjunctive (כִּֽי). There can be no question that the latter is correct. It emphasises the *reasons*, advanced by Eli, for his somewhat tardy expostulation with his sons. In order to give effect to an otherwise feeble remonstrance, a distinctive rather than a connective accent is required. "Nay, my sons; *for* it is no good report that I hear: ye make the Lord's people to transgress." The LXX translation, μὴ δουλεύειν, points to the verb עבד ("to serve") instead of עבר ("to transgress"): yet the Masoretic Text is much more expressive. Not to serve God in a sacred office is ominous enough; but to pervert men, or cause the people of Jehovah to backslide, is not less so. It is a crime like that of Lucifer :—

Still, what's your hurt to mine, of doing hurt,
Of hating, tempting, and so ruining?
This sword's *hilt* is the sharpest, and cuts through
The hand that wields it.[1]

Hence the evil wrought by Hophni and Phinehas
was at least three things in one :—

1. *A public scandal :* Eli heard of their evil dealings
   from all the people (ver. 23).
2. *A cause of stumbling to Israel :* they made the
   Lord's people to transgress (ver. 24).
3. *A sin against God :* if a man sin against the Lord,
   who shall intreat for him ? (ver. 25).

Dilatory, as he was, in reproof, the indulgent
father had still a true insight into the character
of moral evil. Beginning in the outer court of
public morality, he tracks it into the holiest of
all, that *there*, in the felt presence of the Eternal,
the sinner may be constrained to cry, like a later
psalmist—

Against thee, thee only, have I sinned,
And done that which is evil in thy sight.

Ps. li. 4.

In this case, however, expostulation was in vain.
The sons refused to follow.

[1] E. B. Browning.

CHAPTER IX

Paseq

THE term " Paseq " is not found in any part of
Scripture, but is derived from a post-biblical
root signifying " to cut off" or " separate ". It
consists of a small perpendicular line placed
between two words, as, אלהים ׀ לאור (Gen. i. 5):
and is of very frequent occurrence in the Hebrew text, appearing no fewer than 95 times
in Genesis alone. But it is not necessary to
enter into all the distinctions that the grammarian or accentuator has introduced in connection with the sign. To say that the same
collocation of symbols (׀ ֥) may be called *L'gar-
meh* or *Munach-Paseq*, according as it appears
before the accent R'bhia or not, may be of some
interest to the Hebrew specialist, but it is of no
practical value to the expositor of God's word.
As foretone to R'bhia it may well have expressed
a stronger melody than it does before any other
accent; but since this musical distinction (whatever it was) can no longer be discovered by us,

the difference between the two names may safely
be disregarded.   The same remark applies to the
distinction between great and small *Shalshéleth*
(especially in the poetical books).   It is called the
former when it is accompanied by Paseq, as,
וּכְבוֹדִ֔י (Ps. vii. 6), וַיֹּאמַ֔ר (Amos. i. 2) ; but
as we never speak of great Mer'kha, great Azla,
etc., when these accents happen to be followed
by the same sign, there is nothing to be gained
by introducing a different nomenclature in the
case of Shalshéleth.   For practical purposes these
superfine distinctions may be left on one side,
and our attention directed simply to the position
and usages of Paseq.

1. Its Position

As already stated, it is inserted between two
words in line with the Hebrew consonants, and
not placed above or below the line like the other
graphical signs.   This raises the question whether
it is to be regarded as an integral part of Hebrew
accentuation.   The generally accepted view is inclined to answer this question in the affirmative.
Paseq may not be classed along with the other
accents, as if equal to them in every particular,
but its influence is so inwoven with the texture
of Hebrew composition, that it is useless to try

and unravel its ever-varying applications apart
from the principles that regulate the present
accentual system. It was remarked, for instance, at the beginning of Chap. VIII., that
after the last of the distinctives had been placed
in position, no fewer than five servi might be required to complete the accentuation. But what
if among these conjunctive accents there should
occur one or more logical pauses ? Was there no
available means of indicating their presence save
through the invention of additional graphical
signs ? There was. The punctuator could always
introduce a sufficient pause in the reading by
means of the simple sign Paseq. *Cf.* 2 Kings
xviii. 14. Here we have a case of six servi being
required at the commencement of the verse : and
it is not difficult for any one who is not colour-
blind or music-deaf to feel that at all the
three places where Paseq is used, there is a
measure of emphasis so pronounced that it demands something more than a conjunctive accent
to mark it. Even our English version, with its
far less flexible system of notation has had to
punctuate it at two different places, in order to
do justice to the reading. "Hezekiah King of
Judah sent to the King of Assyria to Lachish,
saying, I have sinned ; etc." Whether the accentuator invented the sign for this purpose, or

found it ready to his hand in the Hebrew text, is a minor consideration. What *is* important is, that it was now being used for the sake of giving effect to the reading: and this, from the standpoint of biblical exposition, is the one thing that gives meaning and value to the sign.

Dr. Kennedy in his elaborate study, *The Note-Line in Hebrew,* has tried to turn the edge of this by propounding the thesis that Paseq has little or nothing to do with the principles of Hebrew accentuation. It was no more than a simple and primitive expedient for calling attention to what the Sopherim or scribes considered a noteworthy reading. Just as we are accustomed to insert *sic* at a point in a quotation which we do not care to alter, but which we strongly suspect of containing some error; so did these early transcribers employ Paseq to mark the readings which they did not venture to correct, though they entertained a strong suspicion of their incorrectness. The sign, therefore, considered in itself, possessed no distinctively separative force, but was simply a *nota bene* addressed to the eye of the reader reminding him that there was something anomalous or peculiar in the form or construction of the words. But this means that when we come to a passage like Deut. vii. 6,

and read "Thee hath the Lord *chosen* (בָּחַר ')
to be to him a special people;" and find the
note-line inserted at the word "chosen," we are
completely at a loss to account for it. For
there is nothing anomalous or peculiar about the
word in this text; and therefore the appearance
of Paseq as an index to some irregularity is altogether inexplicable. Yet surely any one who has
an ear for the music of spoken words, or spiritual
instinct to feel the depth of meaning in this truly
theocratic phrase, will not demur to any mark of
emphasis by which the Masorete has thought fit
to signalise the reading; but will rejoice that in
the exposition of the divine message he has so
valuable a guide to the understanding of the verse.

The difference between the two ways of regarding Paseq is not so serious as it looks. The
contention that it was introduced by the Sopherim
in pre-Christian times, and that its origin and
purpose were lost in the mists of the past, when
the Masoretes came to invent the dual system of
punctuation, may or may not be the true explanation of the fact; but irrespective of this
altogether, its present position in the Masoretic
scheme must be investigated and valued independently. For what was the state of affairs
when we come to the close of the seventh century

A.D. ? According to Dr. Kennedy the accentuators only made confusion worse confounded by
accepting the note-line as they found it in the
Hebrew text and working it into their own plan.
They took account of the line "wherever it
occurred, as if it were a factor to be considered
in applying their system of signs" (p. 11).
Here then is the precise difference between the
two modes of estimating Paseq. The one believes
that it existed for centuries before the age of the
accentuators, and that its original purpose and
function having been forgotten or misunderstood,
it was taken up and worked into the accentual
system. The other, represented by Dr. Wickes,
is equally convinced that the origin of the
graphical sign came at the *close* of the accentual
period, but was invented and utilised for the
same purpose, *viz.* : to eke out the deficiencies
of the accentual scheme. So that in either case,
it is a factor to be reckoned with in Hebrew
accentuation ; and the distinction between the
two ways of appraising the value of Paseq is reduced to a minimum. The result is that when
both parties come to deal with passages like
Job xiv. 19, 2 Kings v. 11, the one is as eager as
the other to do justice to the emphatic character
of the sign.

אֲבָנִים׳ שָׁחֲקוּ מַיִם

(Even) *stones* the waters wear away.

"But Naaman was wroth, and went away, and said, Behold, I thought, he will surely come out *to me*" (אֵלַי׳ יֵצֵא יָצוֹא). Hence our former statement regarding the origin and purpose of Paseq may be allowed to stand unaltered. It was used to indicate a slight pause between the words which, after the verse had been arranged musically, were found to be joined together by connective accents. In fine, it virtually changed the conjunctive accent with which it was associated into a minor disjunctive; and proved itself, in the hands of the Masoretes, to be possessed of a distinctively separative force.

2. Its Usages

Allusion has been made already to the chief use of this graphical sign. It was introduced for the sake of *emphasis*. All the other shades of meaning traceable in its various applications, are only so many varying aspects of this same central idea. In Dr. Wickes' language, "The examples under this head are sufficiently numerous, indeed so much so, that we may regard this emphatic use as the chief object of the ordinary Paseq". Take, for instance, the statement in

9

Josh. xxiii. 10. "One man of you shall chase a thousand : *for* (כִּי) the Lord your God, he it is that fighteth for you." This is one of the passages which Dr. Kennedy finds exceptional and embarrassing; for why should the note-line appear before "the Lord your God," when there is nothing anomalous or peculiar in the construction of the words? The explanation is that Paseq does not occur with these words at all ; but with the particle כִּי, and emphasises the basis of Joshua's confidence in the future success of Israel's cause. No foe would be able to withstand the onset of their arms, *for* Jehovah, the God of battles, would be their champion. Even one man with God would be in the majority ; and a stone cast in His name would become a thunderbolt. In short, the *human success* in Athnach's clause is made dependent upon the *divine co-operation* in Silluq's; and Paseq is brought in to emphasise the connection. Who shall say, in view of this connection, that the instinct of the Masorete was at fault? It was no more at fault than when he added in verse 12 : "*Else* (כִּי) if ye do in any wise go back . . . know for a certainty that the Lord your God will no more drive these nations from out of your sight ". It is like the rapier-thrust in Gen.

iv. 7 : "*If* thou doest not well, sin coucheth at
the door ".

It is only a slight variation of the same
principle when Paseq is used between two words
which end and begin with the same letter, as
מָל , שָׁבְעִים (Judg. i. 7), גַּן ׀ נָעוּל (Cant. iv.
12).   Still the exceptions to this rule are so
numerous that Dr. Wickes is led to the conclusion that even in this position the failure of
Paseq, and not its presence, is the leading
characteristic.   *Cf.* שָׁמַע עַבְדְּךָ (1 Sam. xxiii.
11), לֹא־תֹאכַל לֶחֶם (1 Kings, xiii. 17).   Consequently to speak of distinct pronunciation as
the determining factor in these instances is not
sufficient : it is distinctness of utterance *plus*
logical or musical effect.   The accentuator desired
to impress upon the words something of the conviction he himself felt regarding their significance, and this element of emphasis is not to be
overlooked when we come to analyse their teaching.   Turn, for example, to the statement in
Cant. iv. 12 :—

> A *garden* shut up is my sister, my bride ;
> A *spring* shut up, a fountain sealed.

The LXX has κῆπος, a garden, in both clauses ;
and we may probably have to read :—

גַּן, נָעוּל אֲחֹתִי כַלָּה
גַּן נָעוּל מַעְיָן חָתוּם:

It is no argument against this that the first גַּן
is marked by Paseq, whereas the second is left
unaccented; for the emphasis impressed upon the
first clause has given sufficient prominence to
the striking metaphor, and when once the nail
has been driven home, it serves no good purpose
to split the wood.

One other variation of the same usage may be
mentioned. Paseq is frequently employed (especially in the poetical books) to conserve the
sanctity of the Divine name. At every stage in
the history of the text, this feeling of reverence
has made itself felt. Even in the time of the
Sopherim, as observed in Chap. II., it was allowed
to modify the Hebrew *consonants* (1 Sam. iii.
13, Job vii. 20, etc.). In the later period of the
Masoretes it exerted a similar influence in determining the *vowels*. *Cf.* Isa. i. 12, where instead
of the expression " to see my face," we are asked
to read " to appear before me " (*i.e.,* לֵרָאוֹת for
לִרְאוֹת). The former expression was deemed too
anthropomorphic to apply to the Deity; and
therefore despite the difficulty of construing פָּנַי

as an accusative with the Niphal, the vocalisation was altered to suit their preconceived views (Ex. xxxiv. 24). And now the same feeling of scrupulosity is to be allowed to influence Hebrew *accentuation*. By the use of what has been called *Paseq euphemisticum* the Divine name is to be safeguarded whenever it comes into proximity with that which was not considered becoming. It was not thought seemly, for instance, to speak of the "wicked" in the same breath with the name of the Deity; and therefore when we come to passages like Ps. x. 13, cxxxix. 21, and read:—

> Wherefore doth the wicked contemn God?
>
> . . . .
>
> Do not I hate them, O Lord, that hate thee?
>
> . . . .

we must punctuate them as follows:—

נִאֵץ רָשָׁע ׀ אֱלֹהִים

מְשַׂנְאֶיךָ יְהוָה ׀ אֶשְׂנָא

And in a similar manner if anything derogatory to the Divine being could not be emended otherwise, by rearrangement of the consonants or vowels, the difficulty could always be surmounted by the insertion of an euphemistic Paseq. *Cf.* Ps. xliv. 24:—

Awake, why sleepest thou, O Lord ?

The ascription of sleep to the Holy One of Israel
was not considered becoming by these devout
scholars ; and the feeling of incongruity was duly
marked by the insertion of the graphical sign :—

עוּרָה‧ לָמָּה תִישַׁן‧ אֲדֹנָי

Here again we have simply another application of the same principle which we have
found so often in the accentual scheme. It was
a system which addressed itself to the task of
indicating the relation—logical or otherwise—
of each word in the sentence ; and it could not
be conceived as overlooking any shade of emphasis that sought to find expression either in
written symbol or in spoken word. It might
be the depth of the thought, the weight of the
melody, the fulness of the emotion or the throb
of the moral sense, but in either case the tone or
stress was not neglected. It was marked by
Paseq ; and the sign as thus employed was the
expression of a distinctively separative force.

3. Two Practical Illustrations

"And God created man in his own image, in
the image of God created he him : male and
female created he them" (Gen. i. 27). The main

logical pause is rightly placed at *him*, for at
this point the verse falls asunder into two parts,
containing (*a*) man's relation to God, and (*b*)
man's relation to woman.   These are the two
natural divisions of the verse.   A minor distinctive, Zaqeph, is then placed at *image*, dividing the clause of Athnach into the two members
of a clearly expressed parallelism.   This leaves
Zaqeph's own clause to be subdivided at *man*
by its musical foretone Pashta.   Thus :—

וַיִּבְרָא אֱלֹהִים ׀ אֶת־הָאָדָם בְּצַלְמוֹ ׀

What is the force of Paseq at Elohim ?   With
a minor dichotomy on the first word before
Pashta, we might expect a distinctive accent,
like Geresh before R'bhia ; but as a rule, transformation takes place into the corresponding
servus, and then the secution in Pashta's clause
becomes Azla, M'huppakh, Pashta (*cf.* Gen. xliii.
3).   What then is the significance of the sign
Paseq ?   It is the key to the whole passage.   The
text is not simply a description of the creation of
man : it is a statement of the *Divine idea* in
man's creation.   From ver. 1 the name "Elohim" has been carried, like a lamp, through
the entire chapter, and every clause and phrase
is illumined with its light.   In the divine plan,

man was meant to be the head of all created things—creation's mouth-piece and nature's high priest (ver. 26); so that a threefold division is set before us in these two verses—

(1) Man's relation to *nature* (ver. 26).

(2) Man's relation to *woman* (ver. 27b).

(3) Man's relation to *God* (ver. 27a).

This is the divine idea in man's creation—an idea which is suitably expressed by the emphatic Paseq: when man left the Creator's hand, he was at once a *natural*, a *moral* and a *spiritual* being.

The preacher will find an equally interesting passage at Prov. iii. 11, 12. The ordinary pointing at the beginning of ver. 12 is, כִּי אֶת אֲשֶׁר, but in various respects this is quite anomalous. It provides more than three servi for Athnach which is most unusual, and it points אֶת with S'gol which is only permissible when it is joined to the following word by Maqqeph. These difficulties prepare us for the pointing of Ben-Naphtali (כִּי אֶת־אֲשֶׁר) which furnishes another instructive example of an emphatic Paseq :—

> My Son, despise not the chastening of the Lord :
> Neither be weary of his reproof :
> *For* whom the Lord loveth he reproveth ;
> Even as a father the son in whom he delighteth.

Thus interpreted, the change suggests a suitable line of exposition for dealing with the subject of divine discipline, *viz.* : the various *reasons* advanced in these two verses for not despising the chastening of the Lord.

(1) *The making of the man.* This is the precise meaning of the term "chastening". It means the removing of flaws or faults by the process of correction (chap. xxii. 15). If men would but consent to be made! "whereas, behaving like children who struggle and scream while their mother washes and dresses them, they find they have to be washed and dressed notwithstanding, and with the more discomfort; they may even have to find themselves set half-naked and but half-dried in a corner and ask to be finished".[1]

(2) *The aggravating of the discipline.* Is this not the thought suggested by the term "reproof"? The ordinary voice of instruction has to give place to the more peremptory accents of rebuke : and the moulding and refining process has to be done all over again—a consideration which gives peculiar fitness to the term "weary". "Neither be weary of his reproof."

(3) *The verifying of a father's love.* A father does not correct the faults of a servant as he

---

[1] *Sir Gibbie.*

corrects the faults of a child. He may be content to get rid of the former, but, if possible, he
has to make a man of the latter; and therefore
he trains, counsels and disciplines him as such.
The ills of life are no proof that the father has
forgotten him: they are chastisement the proof
of his love (*cf.* Heb. xii. 6). So that reading these
three thoughts together, the man will not rebel
against the refining and perfecting process. He
will believe that a father's love knows best what
is necessary for him; and having been brought
to a right frame of mind by the discipline through
which he has been passing, he will draw near to
the divine footstool, like the child drawing near
to his mother, and ask *to be finished*. This is the
sum of the whole matter: love seeks the final
perfecting of the man.

CHAPTER X

It was suggested in Chap. III. that the poetical
accentuation was simply a refinement of the
Palestinian Schools, introduced to secure a richer
melody in the chanting of the three books.
By means of a fuller intonation, they sought to
compensate for the shortness of the verse, in
Psalms, Proverbs, and Job. And this terseness
in poetic composition explains another feature
of the system. There was no necessity for the
same number of minor distinctives as are found
in the larger clauses of the twenty-one prose
books. The main distinctives are much the same,
in number and function ; but when we come to
the sub-divisions, and note the accents which
are used to mark them, the list is a good deal
shorter than in the corresponding prose list.
Instead of the three accents, Zaqeph, Tiphcha
and R'bhia, we have to be content with two,
R'bhia Mugrash which in some respects is the
counterpart of Tiphcha, and simple *R'bhia* which

141

corresponds in great measure to its namesake in
the prose accentuation. Then with regard to the
lighter distinctives, Pashta, T'bhir and Zarqa,
we have to be satisfied with two again—*D'chi*,
which may be considered as discharging the
functions of Pashta and T'bhir, and *Şinnor*
which performs a similar duty in relation to
Zarqa. Until in passing to the distinctives of
least degree, Geresh, Pazer, and Great T'lisha, and
comparing the accentual divisions in the three
books, we find no more than one disjunctive, the
accent *Pazer*, unless we add the various combinations of *Paseq*, which frequently indicates,
as in the prose books, a slight logical or musical
pause. In fine, the prose accentuation requires
no fewer than nine minor distinctives to accomplish what the poetic system can achieve with
five, or at the most six : so that there is some
justification for the opinion that in several particulars the poetic notation is the simpler of the
two ; and that in any case, the two systems
may be studied side by side. In the present
instance, we limit our attention to the two leading distinctives, Olev'yored and Athnach.

1. Their Names

The term Athnach has been sufficiently explained in Chap. V., but the name *Olev'yored*

(עוֹלֶה וְיוֹרֵד) calls for some additional remark.
It means the "ascending and descending" modulation. The upper sign is like M'huppakh, and
is placed *above* and *before* the tone-syllable; so
that if the tone be on the first syllable of the
word, the M'huppakh is thrown back on the previous word, as יַרְאֵנוּ טוֹב (Ps. iv. 7). But if
the previous word be accented on the ultima,
this retrocession of the sign cannot take place;
we must read וְיִשַׁר אָתָּה (Job viii. 6). Even in
this case, however, Baer makes no difference in
his text—he points it וְיִשַׁר אָתָּה; while his
treatment of שׁוּב נָא (Ps. lxxx. 15) is still more
striking—he writes שׁוּב נָא.

The *servant* to Olev'yored is *Galgal,* a "wheel"
—a name which was probably suggested by its
original circular form. But sometimes, for the
sake of emphasis, a distinctive may be required
on the first word before Olev'yored; and then,
both in thought and in expression, the weight of
the reading must not be overlooked in the fram-
ing of the translation. *Cf.* Prov. xxiii. 35 :—

> They have stricken me, and I was not hurt ;
> They have *beaten* me, and I felt it not.

Here the main pause before Olev'yored is on

hurt ; and as this is the second word before that
accent, it is rightly marked by Ṣinnor. In this
case however, the intervening word should have
Galgal the ordinary servant to Olev'yored (*cf.*
Ps. vii. 9). With this accentuation the two clauses
would have been exactly parallel, the initial verbs
being joined to the following by connective accents. Thus :—

$$\text{הִכּוּנִי בַל־חָלִיתִי}$$
$$\text{הֲלָמוּנִי בַל־יָדָעְתִּי}$$

But this would have missed the thought already
expressed by the well-chosen Hebrew verbs.
נָכָה in the Hiphil means to smite by a single
blow, as when Saul sought to pin David to the
wall by one throw of his spear (1 Sam. xix. 10);
whereas הָלַם has the further idea of smiting with
a hammer (הַלְמוּת), like the smith striking the
anvil in Isa. xli. 7, or Jael driving home the
tent-pin by repeated blows of her mallet (Jud. v.
26). To be smitten once by strong drink and not
feel the wound is ominous enough : but there is
a deeper degradation than that. The drunkard's
path is downward. Everything is burned up in
that liquid ' fire; until in a condition of moral
imbecility he wails, " They have beaten me (over

and over again) and I felt it not : when shall I awake ? I will seek it yet again ". This is the full force of the distinctive *R'bhia* which the Masoretes have introduced instead of the servant Galgal. Both lexicon and music have been requisitioned to emphasise the truth that the wages of sin is death.

2. Their Position

Olev'yored, in the poetic books, may be brought into comparison with S'golta in the prose. They agree in this, that if a strong pausal accent is required in addition to Athnach, it is marked in prose by S'golta, and in the three books by Olev'yored. But unlike S'golta, Olev' yored is not to be regarded as subordinate to Athnach. If both accents are required in the same verse, it is the former and not the latter which indicates the main dichotomy, as,

> Many sorrows shall be to the wicked : $(\overline{}\llcorner)$
> But he that trusteth in the Lord, $(\overline{}_\Delta)$
> Mercy shall compass him about.
>
> (Ps. xxxii. 10).

Hence the prosaic and poetic systems may be compared thus :—

$$: \overline{} \text{- - - - - - -} \parallel \overline{}_\Delta \text{- - - - - ⋅ -} \mid \overset{..}{\overline{}} \text{- - - - - }\}$$
$$: \overline{} \text{- - - - - - - } \mid \overline{}_\Delta \text{- - - - - - } \parallel \overline{}\llcorner \text{- - - - - }\}$$

In both notations the verse was divided into
two parts, and one of the parts sub-divided by
means of a subordinate accent : but while in the
prose system it is the first section that is so
dealt with, the poetic accentuation subdivides
the second.   There are many passages, of course,
where Olev'yored does not appear at all.   Owing
to the shortness of the verses there was no need
for the introduction of both accents : and in fact,
within Psalms, Proverbs, and Job, Athnach
marks the main dichotomy at least ten times as
often as Olev'yored.   The rule is that if the
cæsura falls on the first, second, or third word
before Silluq, it is sufficiently well-marked by
Athnach (*cf.* the whole of Ps. ii., with the exception of ver. 7).   If it fall on the fourth or
fifth, the usage fluctuates between Athnach and
Olev'yored ; but on the sixth word or further,
the dichotomy is always marked by Olev'yored.
In Ps. ii. 7, for instance, the main pause falls on
the eighth word before Silluq ; and since another
fairly strong pause falls between it and the close
of the verse, it is accented and pointed accordingly.

I will tell of the decree : ($\smile$)
The Lord said unto me, Thou art my son ; ($\overline{\wedge}$)
This day have I begotten thee.

These general divisions are well illustrated by
Ps. c. 3—especially as read with the *Q'ri* (לוֹ)
instead of the *K'thibh* (לֹא).

> Know ye that the Lord he is God :
> It is he that hath made us, *and we are his ;*
> We are his people, and the sheep of his pasture.

The mere fact that they have been chosen of God
and welded into a nation, was the historical and
redemptive basis on which their knowledge of
Jehovah was to be settled.   It was in this sense
that He had *made* them, and called them into
fellowship with Himself ; and therefore they
were His—they were His people and He was
their God.   The main pause is consequently
placed at *God* ; for there the injunction to know
Jehovah, as Elohim, ends, and the proof of His
deity begins.   In other words, the whole verse is
a case of partial parallelism, in which the leading
thought is expressed in the first two lines with
the cæsura between them : and then a third line
has been added in order to expand the concluding portion of the second member.   Within these
general divisions another fairly strong pause is
placed on *know* and *made,* as if to emphasise the
means by which the enjoyment of this communion is to be attained.   It is by knowledge—
the knowledge of the heart—that man comes to

find his portion in Jehovah, and it is by a similar outputting of the divine energy— in knowing, choosing, making—that Jehovah comes to find His portion in His people (*cf.* the use of יָדַע "to know," in Gen. xviii. 19, Amos iii. 2). Hence the divisions of our subject are obvious.

(1) The knowledge that finds a God.

(2) The Divine working that finds a people.

(3) The happy issue—a Shepherd and his flock.

3. Their Musical Character

As might be expected from the more rhyth-mical accentuation of the three books, the pre-sence of the melody has a much greater influence in Psalms, Proverbs and Job than it has in the twenty-one prose books. The logical and syn-tactical divisions are far more frequently sacrificed to the claims of musical equilibrium. Especially is this the case when the dichotomy would fall after the first, or before the last word of the verse. It is shifted forwards or backwards to a more convenient resting-place, so as to preserve more adequately the balance of the modulation (*cf.* Job iv. 8). In his early volume on "Job," Professor Davidson was of opinion that the participles

חרשי and זרעי were *not* accusatives after "I
have seen," but nominatives to the verb "to reap";
and therefore ought to be rendered, as in the
English version, "As I have seen, they that plow
iniquity, and sow wickedness, reap the same". In
the *Cambridge Bible*, however, he is not so positive
on this point; and is prepared to admit that the
words may also read, "When I saw those that
ploughed iniquity and sowed trouble, they reaped
it". In either case, the leading distinctive is not
placed at "trouble," where the main logical pause
requires it, but at "iniquity," so as to preserve
the principle of musical equilibrium. The two
expressions, to plough iniquity and to sow trouble
are parallel to each other; and are therefore suitably separated by the caesura. It is melody, however, and not logic that has determined the accentuation. In order to exhibit *parallelismus
membrorum* the logical and syntactical division
has had to give way.

If it did not seem possible to the accentuators
to change the position of the dichotomy—deterred,
it may be, by the shortness of the verse or some
similar consideration—they surmounted the difficulty in another way. They marked the main
logical pause by a minor distinctive. In place of
Athnach which was too heavy an accent for the
first word before Silluq they introduced R'bhia

Mugrash (Job iv. 1, Ps. xxxiv. 8), and instead
of Olev'yored or Athnach at the beginning of the
verse, especially after the addition of some super-
scription, they used Paseq with Azla, or Pazer
(Ps. xxv. 1, xxvi. 1). It did not seem consistent
with the claims of the modulation to insert so
strong an accent in these short verses; and therefore like the use of Zaqeph in Hab. i. 1, the
dichotomy was sufficiently well-marked by one
of the lighter accents.

> Hear instruction, and be wise, (*R. Mugrash*).
> And refuse it not (Prov. viii. 33).

As a noteworthy illustration of the main distinctives see Ps. xlv. 5. The A.V. renders, "Thine
arrows are sharp in the heart of the King's
enemies: whereby the people fall under thee".
This is a most inadequate rendering of the Masoretic accentuation. The greatest pause is at
sharp; for here the description of the conqueror
ends, and the picture of the vanquished begins.
It is therefore marked by Olev'yored. The
next greatest pause is at *thee,* and the final
stop at *King,* so that we ought to read as in
the R.V. :—

> Thine arrows are sharp :
> Peoples fall under thee ;
> In the heart of the enemies of the King.

Does it need a strong imagination, asks Professor Davidson, to see a whole campaign here—the preparation, the conflict, the victory? A warrior stalking into the field with sharpened weapons, the same mowing down nations, and then the battlefield filled with slain, each with a well-aimed javelin in his heart. In Dr. Maclaren's fine language, the conqueror has no allies. The canvas has no room for soldiers. The picture is like the Assyrian sculptures, in which the King stands erect and alone in his chariot, a giant in comparison with the tiny figures beneath him. Like Rameses in Pentaur's great battle-song, "he pierced the line of the foe: . . . he was all alone, no other with him". And so thoroughly have the Masoretes entered into the spirit of this passage, that they have even dispensed with one of the commonest rules of their prosody, viz.: that under Athnach there must be a long and pausal vowel. In order to express the rapidity and almost terrified breathlessness with which the last two exclamations are uttered, they allow the verb יִפָּלוּ to appear with simple sheva. [1] The men who could paint a scene like this, with such delicacy and finish, are worth knowing. They were masters of their craft.

---

[1] Davidson's *Accentuation*, p. 49.

Finally, in Ps. cii. 3, the LXX suggests a different grouping of the main distinctives as compared with the Masoretic Text. It reads :—

> Turn not thy face away from me :
> In the day of my distress, incline thine ear unto me ;
> In the day when I call upon thee, answer me speedily.

For various reasons this arrangement is to be preferred. It not only discloses a marked antithesis between the two parts of the psalmist's prayer (the negative, " turn not," and the positive, " incline unto "); it shows also in the latter or positive portion a good example of progressive parallelism. The *silent appeal* of his distress rests, for an interval, in the equally *silent attitude* of Jehovah; but ere long it breaks forth into the eloquence of a *verbal entreaty*, that the divine attitude may express itself in *action*, and that a speedy answer may be granted to his request. In the day of his distress he prays at least for three things :—

1. The divine nearness—(1st line).
2. The divine interest—(2nd line).
3. The divine interposition—(3rd line).

" In the day when I call, answer me speedily."

CHAPTER XI

THE MINOR DISTINCTIVES (POETICAL)

IN both systems of notation, and in comparatively short verses, the main distinctive, as already noted, may not appear at all (*cf.* Job iii. 1-2). The prologue and epilogue of this dramatic poem are accented according to the ordinary prose system; so that in these two verses the characteristics of the two parallel schemes are found side by side. In either case, the main dichotomy is sufficiently emphasised by one of the minor distinctives—by Zaqeph in the one instance, and R'bhia Mugrash in the other— a clear indication that however different the graphical signs may be, the same accentual law is operative in both. In the present section we shall limit our inquiry to the three minor distinctives—R'bhia Mugrash, D'chi and Sinnor.

1. R'BHIA MUGRASH (מְגֻרָשׁ ʼר)

This accent has a two-fold graphical sign because, in early times, it had probably a two-fold

modulation.   The first part is a simple stroke,
not unlike the Geresh of the prose accentuation,
and placed above and on the right hand of the
initial letter; while the second and more important part is an ordinary R'bhia, which is used,
like the accents generally, to indicate the tone-
syllable.   The resemblance to Geresh explains
the meaning of the name, R'bhia Mugrash, *i.e.*,
R'bhia *gereshed*—the מְגֹרָשׁ being Pual participle
of גרש.   Rabbinical writers, however, preferred
the name Tiphcha, not simply because the stroke
in question was probably nothing more than the
Tiphcha-sign of the prose books transferred from
below, but also and especially because R'bhia
Mugrash occupies the same position before Silluq
as Tiphcha does in the prose accentuation.   *Cf.*
the first verse in Job's opening speech :—

יֹאבַד יֹום אִוָּלֶד בֹּו

וְהַלַּיְלָה אָמַר הֹרָה גָבֶר :

Here, R'bhia Mugrash marks the one dichotomy
in Silluq's clause, and is preceded by its ordinary
servus Mer'kha.   But the verse is interesting in
other respects, and is to be noted both from the
side of grammar and accentuation.   The A.V.
renders the second line " the night in which it

was said," as if אָמַר were a passive form of the
verb like אוּלַד before Athnach; but the R.V.
has at once preserved the grammar of the word,
and restored the poetry of the verse, by recog-
nising הַלַּיְלָה as personified, and reading "the
night which said". It was the night itself, and
not any human herald of the event, that first
announced the fact that a man child had been
born into the world. The further distinction
that the day refers to his birth, and the night to
his conception, is a subtilty that may have
attraction for some minds; but probably we
ought to read with the LXX Ἰδοὺ ἄρσεν,
"Behold a male," *i.e.*, הִנֵּה instead of הֹרָה—an
expression that has no reference to conception,
but merely to fruitfulness. The one thought
the patriarch wishes to express is not, that night
played one part, and day another, in the earliest
stages of his existence, but that under the
parallelism or contrast of day and night, he
seeks to give adequate expression to the cry,
"Would God I had never been born!"

> Perish the day wherein I was born,
> And the night which said, Behold a male.

The student will also note in אוּלַד בּוֹ an illustration of the rule that when two accented

syllables come together, the tone of the former
is retracted to the penult to allow a sufficient
hiatus between the two.

The above is the usual position of Silluq's
foretone; and were it not for the law of transformation which exerts so powerful an influence
in the three books, R'bhia Mugrash would be
found in every instance where any kind of dichotomy has entered into Silluq's clause. But its
absence, and not its presence, is the leading characteristic. There is no lack of instances like
Job iii. 4, where the musical foretone has been
changed into a servus on the first word before
Silluq :—

וְאַל־תּוֹפַע עָלָיו נְהָרָה׃

Here the final accent seems to be preceded by
two servi—Ṭarcha and Munach—but the Munach
is really a transformed R'bhia Mugrash on the
first word before Silluq; and therefore the two
servi have a closer affinity to one another than
the Munach has to Silluq.

The advantage of this transformation was that
it gave a greater variety to the modulation of
the three books. There is no question, however,
that it mars, in no slight degree, the order and
symmetry of the accentual system. In the reading

of the clause, the dichotomy has to be reckoned with, whether expressed or not: so that wherever two or more servi are found before Silluq, a slight pause is to be made in the reading on the last servus before the final accent, as Ps. cxix. 86 :—

שֶׁקֶר רְדָפוּנִי עָזְרֵנִי׃

> They persecute me wrongfully, help thou me.

On one condition only does the minor distinctive remain even on the first word before Silluq. If Silluq's own word is sufficiently long—if it contains two or more syllables before the tone, a sufficient interval exists between the two distinctives, and the transformation of R'bhia Mugrash into the corresponding servus does not take place. *Cf.* עָמָל מֵעֵינָי׃ (Job iii. 10). Or for a practical illustration observe the closing words of Job xxiv. 13 :—

> These are of them that rebel against the light;
> They know not the ways thereof,
> Nor abide in the paths thereof.

Carey has referred with justice to John iii. 20, for while "the light" is best understood of the light of day, the implication is that the workers of iniquity love the darkness rather than the light because their deeds are evil. This agrees with

the LXX which frequently gives a paraphrase of
the words instead of a literal translation.

ὁδὸν δὲ δικαιοσύνης οὐκ ᾔδεισαν.

And they know not the way of *righteousness*.

The passage, however, will repay careful study
in other respects. The first word, "these," is
emphatic, referring to the kind of men whom the
speaker is about to describe—the murderer (v.
14), the adulterer (v. 15) and the robber (v. 16);
and therefore it is marked by an emphatic Paseq.
Again, the words accented by Olev'yored are
given by Theile with Metheg and Maqqeph instead of Galgal; and Ginsburg, while omitting
the Maqqeph, has retained the Metheg; but as
Galgal is the ordinary servus of Olev'yored, Baer
and Wickes have corrected it into בְּמַרְדֵי אוֹר.

Finally we have the important verb יְשֻׁבּוּ accented by the minor distinctive R'bhia Mugrash:
"They *abide* not in the paths thereof". The sin
of the rebels was *practical* infidelity. It was
not simply the fruit of ignorance (second line),
or unwillingness to recognise the ways of righteousness; but the unwillingness, in turn, was the
outcome of evil practices, or the walking in the
paths of wickedness. The tap-root was something palpable. A wicked, careless life had led

to a disposition which was reluctant to acknow-
ledge the right; and this again had issued in an
attitude of open rebellion. Careless indifference,
secret dislike, open hatred—these are the three
stages in the natural history of ungodliness.
What begins with practical infidelity ends at last
with something far more solemn—the insolent
and vindictive opposition of the braggart.

2. D'CHI (דְּחִי)

For the meaning of this name see Chap. VI.
D'chi is simply the Tiphcha of the prose accentuation transferred to the first letter and made
prepositive, in order to distinguish it from the
conjunctive Tarcha which has the same form, but
is placed under the tone. In position it occupies
the same place in Athnach's clause as R'bhia
Mugrash holds in Silluq's. It may be found on
the first or second word before Athnach according
to the rules of the dichotomy : but if the minor
distinctive falls too near the tone of the greater
accent, D'chi is transformed into the corresponding servus, just as in the case of R'bhia Mugrash.
Thus we write :—

חֵלֶק־אָדָם רָשָׁע מֵאֱלֹהִים (Job xx. 29),

where D'chi is allowed to remain, because in

11

Athnach's word two or more syllables intervene between the two distinctives; but:—

חלק־אדם רָשָׁע ׀ עִם־אֵל (xxvii. 13),

a case of transformation, because a sufficient hiatus does not exist before the final accent. In the latter case the melody is allowed to override the logical division of the clause. The sense may require a disjunctive accent, but the melody does not permit it, as,

> Are not my days few ? Cease then.
> (Job x. 20).

For an instructive study in connection with this accent, the preacher may turn to Job xiv. 1 :

> *Man* that is born of a woman
> Is of few days, and full of trouble.

The term "man" is to the whole verse what the verse, in turn, is to the entire paragraph (vers. 1-6). The theme is mortality, its weakness, brevity and sorrow; and as this is pregnantly summarised in the first word אָדָם (LXX, βροτός), it is rightly placed at the head of the clause in a position of emphasis and marked by a disjunctive accent. The main cæsura is found at "woman"; for while, at a first reading, the verse seems to consist of three parallel clauses in apposition to each other, it is not really so. It is only the last two clauses that can be described in this way : the first phrase, "born of a woman" being rather an adjectival clause belonging to the subject "man". Hence it was a true instinct of the Masorete, which led him to mark this distinction by the fixing of the main dichotomy— placing the human origin of man in the one half of the verse, and his leading characteristics in the second.

(1) *His Weakness*—"Born of a woman."

In the higher teaching of the New Testament, that which is born of the flesh is flesh; and thus we have the pathetic longing of ver. 4 : "Would that a clean thing could come out of an unclean!" But alas, the wish is its own answer : "There is none that doeth good, no, not one" (Ps. xiv. 3).

(2) *His Brevity*—"Short of days."

So ver. 2 : "He cometh forth like a flower and *withereth*". We prefer the marginal reading יִמָּל from מָלַל, to wither, not simply because the idea of fading is most appropriate to a flower, but because the LXX read יִבֹּל (ἐξέπεσαν) from נָבֵל, to fade, which was probably the original reading (*cf.* Isa. xl. 7).

(3) *His Sorrow*—" Full of trouble."

He was like the day-labourer working in the
fields, and longing for the quiet of evening when
he would gain a brief respite from his toil (vers.
5, 6). The hireling fulfils his day buoyed up by
the thought of the evening hour of rest (*cf.* vii. 2) ;
and the patriarch craves a similar relaxation. He
hopes that in the evening of life he will be allowed
a brief interval of well-earned rest, before he passes
into the silent land from which there is no return.

Woman-born, short-lived and sorrow-oppressed
man ! "Dost thou open thine *eye* upon such an
one, and bringest *him* into judgment with thee ?"
(ver. 3). Note the singular אֵינֶךָ without the
plural *yod ;* and the LXX אֹתִו instead of אֹתִי.

An equally interesting example may be found
at Prov. iv. 3.

Even the R.V. renders, "For I was a son unto
my father"; but this fails to do justice to the
emphatic pointing and position of the term "son".
The LXX, no less than the Hebrew, suggests a
much more forcible rendering :—

> υἱὸς γὰρ ἐγενόμην κἀγὼ πατρὶ ὑπήκοος
> καὶ ἀγαπώμενος ἐν προσώπῳ μητρός.

A glance at the context will illustrate the nature
of this emphasis, and justify the Masoretic in-

stinct which stamped it with a distinctive accent.
The whole paragraph (vers. 1-9) deals with the
person and work of the religious teacher; and
the delineation may be summarised as follows:—

(i.) *His pupils* (vers. 1, 2). They are represented as an entire class: ver. 1 being the only
passage throughout the first nine chapters, where
the phrase "my son" has been changed into the
plural. Such a teacher may have no children of
his own; but if his heart has been touched by
the humanising influence of heavenly wisdom,
he will seek a class of spiritual children some-
where else. It is not more natural for a star to
shine or a flower to breathe its perfume, than it
is for heaven-taught wisdom to impart itself to
others:—

> Heaven doth with us as we with torches do,
> Not light them for themselves.

(ii.) *His own early training* (ver. 3). This
verse contains "a charming piece of autobio-
graphy" (Horton). The teacher harks back to
his own youth and early training, and indicates
the character of those opening years as an example for his class. For as the order of the
Hebrew words implies and as it is paraphrased
in the LXX his youth had been characterised by
filial reverence and obedience (ὑπήκοος); and as

it is the home-trained who are the advocates of home-training, he sought to make his own experience a chaplet of grace for his pupils:—

> For a *son* was I to my father,
> Tender and only beloved in the sight of my mother.

(iii.) *His message* (ver. 7). In the remainder of the paragraph (vers. 7-9) there is no precept inculcated save one : *viz.* : "get wisdom". How is this ? Because (*a*) only one thing is *needful*. Heavenly wisdom, or Christian love, is the fulfilling of the whole law. Let there be the breathing of divine love into human souls, as in the recent wonderful movement in Wales, and it will do more to solve our grave social problems than all the municipal or ecclesiastical schemes put together. (*b*) Only one thing will *suffice*. The temptations that assail the pupils may be very different from those that harassed the teacher in his youth ; and therefore the old rules are in large measure inadequate, and totally inapplicable to a new social environment. But what then ? The one thing needful is not the enforcing of special rules, which, like reins to the beast of burden, will influence the life by external compulsion ; but the *infusing of the old motive power of heavenly wisdom,* and allowing the new generation to work out its own destiny with fear and trembling. In the one case you may grow fine ivy; but in the other you rear strong, sturdy trees that are able to support themselves by their own roots, and to provide, if need be, a support and shelter for others.

> Wisdom is the principal thing, therefore get wisdom,
> And with all thou hast gotten, get understanding.

3. Ṣinnor (צִנּוֹר)

The form of the graphical sign and the meaning of the name have been explained and illustrated at p. 103. It was made postpositive to distinguish it from the conjunctive Ṣinnorith which has the same form; and when the word is accented on the Penult the sign is repeated (especially in the Baer and Delitzsch texts) to mark the position of the tone-syllable as בָּאָרֶץ. Like Zarqa before the prose S'golta, Ṣinnor is the ordinary dividing accent before Olev'yored. But unlike R'bhia Mugrash before Silluq, or D'chi before Athnach, Ṣinnor can never appear on the first word before the leading accent. If a minor dichotomy be due in that position, it is marked by simple R'bhia, as אֲנִי שָׁכַבְתִּי וָאִישָׁנָה (Ps. iii. 6).

The one position occupied by Ṣinnor is on the

second word before Olev'yored, and may be
followed by R'bhia, or the servant Galgal on the
first. *Cf.* Prov. xxiii. 35 at p. 143, or Ps. i. 3,
where we read :—

וְהָיָה כְּעֵץ שָׁתוּל עַל־פַּלְגֵי מָיִם

> And he shall be like a tree planted by the streams of
> water.

Both Baer and Ginsburg have pointed Job
xxxix. 25 as an example of R'bhia in Athnach's
clause. If accentual emendation, however, is
justified anywhere it is justified in this passage.
The main logical pause is at "Aha"; for at this
point the description of the war-horse, that marvellous creation of virility and fierceness, falls
into the two halves of a clearly expressed parallelism. The third line has merely expanded in
the form of a rather awkward Zeugma the concluding phrase of the second member. The LXX
therefore has divided it thus :—

σάλπιγγος δὲ σημαινούσης λέγει Εὖγε ·
πόρρωθεν δὲ ὀσφραίνεται κ.τ.λ.

But the LXX has done more than reproduce the
correct punctuation : it has suggested a various
reading which may help to relieve the Zeugma
already referred to. Instead of רַעַם שָׂרִים "the
thunder of the captains," it has read בְּרַעַם

" with the leaping" (from the beginning of ver. 24). So that the proposal of Professor Duhm to read בְּרַעַ שָׂרִים as the original text is not without a measure of plausibility, seeing that רֵעַ is used in the same sense in ch. xxxvi. 33. In either case the main cæsura must be placed at הֵאָח, and this, according to the rule of the dichotomy is marked by Olev'yored. Indeed, as Dr. Wickes found in his collation of MSS., this is actually the reading adopted in various important codices—Olev'yored with its servant Galgal, and Ṣinnor with its ordinary servus Mer'kha. Hence we may correct and translate as follows :—

בְּדֵי שׁוֹפָר יֹאמַר הֵאָח וּמֵרָחוֹק יָרִיחַ
מִלְחָמָה בְּרַעַ שָׂרִים וּתְרוּעָה :

At the loudness of the trumpet, he saith, Aha !
And from afar he snuffeth the battle,
With the shouting of the leaders and the tumult.

The servant of Ṣinnor is generally Mer'kha, but if the tone fall on any other syllable than the first, it becomes Munach, as זִבְחֵי אֱלֹהִים in Ps. li. 17 :—

The sacrifices of God are a broken spirit :
A broken and a contrite heart, O God, thou wilt not despise.

The position of Ṣinnor, and its servus, is sufficient to show that it is not the sacrifices as such, but the sacrifices of *God*, which are the real subject of the present paragraph. The thanksgiving conveyed in the peace offering, and the ascending flame of the burnt offering (ver. 16), will only rise to heaven when the sacrifice is arranged and presented by one who is already right with Jehovah. It follows that the true sacrifice is not the animal victim at all, but the man behind it—the spirit that has been broken by penitence and the heart that has been awed by forgiveness. Without these, all other sacrifices are vain; and this includes not the animal victims alone, but many other offerings that are highly esteemed among men—leading the poet to exclaim in his *Recessional* :—

> The tumult and the shouting dies ;
>   The captains and the kings depart:
> *Still stands Thine ancient sacrifice,*
>   *An humble and a contrite heart.*
> Lord God of Hosts, be with us yet
> Lest we forget—lest we forget.
>
> —Kipling.

CHAPTER XII

THE MINOR DISTINCTIVES (*continued*)

JOB xxxvii. 23 is another passage which ought to be emended accentually. In Baer's text it reads—

$$\text{שַׁדַּי לֹא־מְצָאנֻהוּ שַׂגִּיא־כֹחַ}$$

And the A.V. renders "Touching the Almighty, we cannot find him out: he is excellent in power, and in judgment, and in plenty of justice: he will not afflict." But this is a most inadequate rendering of the Masoretic accents. The principal dichotomy is rightly placed at "power"; for here the description of the Deity, who is the real subject of the sentence, is separated into two parts, containing the two complementary attributes of almighty power and super-abounding righteousness. Not power alone, and not righteousness alone, but power and righteousness combined—a combination that has taken Elihu back to his fundamental conception that "God is mighty, and despiseth not any" (xxxvi.

5). The subject is placed first for the sake of emphasis, and therefore ought to be marked, not by a conjunctive accent, but by the disjunctive R'bhia, as in various MSS. collated by Dr. Wickes. Thus „שַׁדַּי לֹא: so that we render,

The Almighty ! we cannot find him out, who is great in power:
And justice and fulness of righteousness he will not wrest.
Therefore do men fear him, etc.

Hence a natural division of our subject would be

(1) The unmeasured compass of God's power.

(2) The assured character of His justice.

(3) Trusting where we cannot trace.

In this concluding chapter we shall glance at the remaining distinctives in the poetic accentuation.

1. R'BHIA

For the meaning and form of this graphical sign see p. 80. It is simply the R'bhia of the prose notation, transferred to a somewhat similar position in the accentuation of the three books. In both systems it is introduced to meet the exigencies of longer clauses than those usually dealt with in ordinary composition. It is never found in Silluq's clause, where an additional dichotomy is generally marked by Paseq; but

both in Athnach's and in Olev'yored's clause it
occurs with the utmost frequency.

The rule in Athnach's clause is not difficult to
follow. If the dichotomy falls on the second
word before Athnach it is usually marked by
D'chi, but in a few instances its place has been
taken by R'bhia, either as a substitute for D'chi
(Job xxiv. 24), or as an expedient for allowing
D'chi to appear on the first word (xiii. 4).
R'bhia's regular place is on the *third* word
before Athnach (xxxix. 1); and should the
dichotomy fall still further back—on the fourth
word or even on the fifth—the minor distinctive
is repeated, as Job vii. 4 :—

אִם־שָׁכַבְתִּי וְאָמַרְתִּי מָתַי אָקוּם

וּמִדַּד־עָרֶב „

> When I lie down, I say,
> When shall I arise ? but the night is long.

Its position in Olev'yored's clause is equally
simple. On the second word before Olev'yored
the dichotomy is marked by Ṣinnor ; but in any
other position, the accent chosen is R'bhia—
Little R'bhia (to use a distinction approved by
Wickes) on the first word, and *Great* R'bhia on
the third or further (Ps. i. 1). Hence the full
secution of Olev'yored's clause would be Olev'-
yored, Little R'bhia, Ṣinnor, Great R'bhia—

though the symmetry of this order is often
marred by the law of transformation. *Cf.* Ps.
lvi. 14, where great R'bhia has been replaced by
Sinnor on the *third* word before Olev'yored,
because, in this case, a sufficient interval would
not have existed between Great and Little R'bhia.

In connection with the accent R'bhia, the
preacher will find an interesting passage in Job
xiv. 7 :—

$$\text{״כִּי יֵשׁ לָעֵץ תִּקְוָה״}$$

The R.V. translates, " For there is hope of a tree,
if it be cut down, that it will sprout again, etc." :
but this does not do justice to the emphatic
character of the Masoretic accentuation. לָעֵץ is
nothing, if not emphatic, and as the main pause
comes on " hope," dividing the whole verse into
the three clauses of a tristich, the emphasis and
arrangement ought not to be overlooked either in
the printing or in the reading : thus—

> For a *tree* hath hope ;
> If it be cut down it will sprout again,
> And the tender branch thereof will not cease.
> . . . *But man dieth*, etc. (ver. 10).

The contrast between the fall of a tree and the
fate of a man is solemn enough in any connection, but who does not feel that the hopelessness

and pathos are greatly increased by putting the
first line categorically, and not hypothetically,
as our Bible does? It is this contrast which has
left its mark on the entire paragraph (vers. 7-12).
The subject is the total extinction of man's life
in death, as contrasted with the comparative
immortality of a tree. And the simile is applied
in two ways. (*a*) Is the tree cut down while its
life is yet young and vigorous? (ver. 7). It is
not on that account bereft of hope. Abundant
sap is still flowing in the stump or roots, and at
the welcome voice of spring, it will rise and
effloresce. Or (*b*) does the tree begin to droop
and decay as if from the feebleness of age? (ver.
8). Even then the sap which is dying out of the
roots, may be replenished by a timely supply of
moisture from without. "Through the scent of
water it will bud, and put forth its boughs like a
new plant" (LXX, νεόφυτον). Carey, in his
Illustrations, refers this to the date-palm, which
is pre-eminently a φιλύδρον φυτόν, and like the
Phœnix whose name it bears (φοῖνιξ) seems to arise
anew from its ashes. But, alas, for the parallel!

> Man dieth, and is laid prostrate,
> Yea, man giveth up the ghost, and where is he?

As well ask where the Arabian stream has gone
—evaporated in the sun and absorbed in the

12

sand (ver. 11). Man has really entered upon his
last sleep. Ver. 12 means *for ever* (*cf.* Jer.
li. 39).

But note the similar emphatic R'bhia in ver.
14 :—

> If a *man* die, shall he live again ?

Is the blank nescience of ver. 12 the final word
on this subject ; or will the patriarch be guided
by his own inextinguishable heart-religion to
pursue, in verses 13-15, the phantom of a better
hope ? The surprising idea has come to the
sufferer that the fate of man may not be so hap-
less as he feared. Man is more than a tree ; and
therefore the *Love* of God which called him into
existence at the first, may yet hark back to its
former mercy, and have a desire to the work of
His hands. True the *Wrath* of God was daily
pursuing and hurrying him to Sheol ; but there
was this other side to the Divine character—a
disposition that longed to triumph over judgment ; and therefore appealing from the one to
the other, from the Wrath to the Love, he ex-
claims, like our own Crashaw :—

> But thou giv'st leave (dread Lord !) that we
> Take shelter from Thyself in Thee ;
> And with the wings of Thine own dove,
> Fly to Thy sceptre of soft love. [1]

[1] See *Ency. Biblica*, col. 2472.

Or the preacher might have turned to a similar emphatic R'bhia in Ps. lxxii. 15 :—

וִיחִי וְיִתֶּן־לוֹ מִזְּהַב שְׁבָא

The A.V. renders " And *he* shall live, and to him shall be given of the gold of Sheba ". But when we turn to the R.V. we are asked to apply the verb וִיחִי to the "poor and needy," who have been pitied and redeemed in verses 12-14. " Precious shall *their* blood be in his sight : and *they* shall live, etc." There is, however, no justification for this emendation either in the LXX or in the Masoretic text. The former reads, after a full stop at *sight, καὶ ζήσεται καὶ δοθήσεται αὐτῷ ἐκ χρυσίου τῆς Ἀραβίας.*—*i.e.*, the precise rendering of the A.V.—and even though a connection does exist between ver. 15 and the previous verses, we submit that in the Hebrew text, it leads to quite a different conclusion from that suggested by the revisers. The subject of the context is none other than Israel's ideal king ; for while the Psalm, in several of its details, has an undoubted reference to some earthly monarch, it is rightly regarded in other particulars as an idealistic picture, which is only satisfied by a distinct allusion to the Messianic fulfilment. By a series of verbs in the *singular*, the services of that ideal king are fitly detailed by the psalmist; while the poor and needy are as suitably repre-sented by the *plural* suffix (םָ‎ָ)—"*their* soul" and "*their* blood" (ver. 14). So that in view of such a context, it does seem somewhat arbitrary, either to translate a singular verb (וִיחִי‎) by "they" instead of "he," or to introduce so radical a change of subject in a word accented by R'bhia. When the way has been prepared for this change by the impersonal verb יִתֶּן‎, there may be some adequate reason for the alteration, especially after so strong an accent as Olev'-yored; but with a subordinate accent like R'bhia the introduction of a new subject is not warranted; and therefore the margin of the R.V. and not the text is to be accepted as the true reading. "And he shall live, and to him shall be given of the gold of Sheba; and men shall pray for him continually; and they shall bless him all the day long." In fine, the favourite division of this text is amply justified, that the church has

    (1) A living Head.
    (2) A liberal hand.
    (3) A praying heart.
    (4) A praising tongue.

2. Pazer and Paseq

The proper function of these two distinctives is to mark the major and minor dichotomies in three different clauses—that of D'chi, Ṣinnor and Great R'bhia : specially Great R'bhia. Thus—

With respect to the *Servi* of these three accents, the usage is anything but uniform in the different passages. R'bhia, for instance, has never more than one servus ; but this may be one of four conjunctives, according as the word is preceded by Paseq or has an open syllable before the tone. In Ps. i. 3, it is pointed with Illuy ($\doteq$), because it is preceded by Azla-Paseq, but in iv. 2 it prefers the pointing M'huppakh with Ṣinnorith, because in addition to Paseq, the word itself has an open syllable directly preceding the tone. When neither Paseq nor Pazer precedes, the servus is almost always M'huppakh, as Ps. ii. 8 ; and in a few instances in which it is preceded by another R'bhia, it may be changed into Mer'kha, as Prov. iv. 4, or Job xxxii. 5, where Wickes points כִּי־אֵין instead of כִּי אֵין.

With but *one dichotomy* in R'bhia's clause, we use Paseq with Azla or Paseq with M'huppakh, as Job iv. 16. But if a minor pause is required, either before or after the main dichotomy, Pazer is used to mark the latter, and Paseq the former, as Ps. vii. 6.

יְרַדֹּף אוֹיֵב ׀ נַפְשִׁי וְיַשֵּׂג

Let the enemy pursue my soul, and overtake it.

These are by far the most common divisions of R'bhia's clause: though we sometimes meet with one or two trifling exceptions, as when two Paseqs are found instead of Pazer and Paseq, on the principle that when the same accent is repeated, it has the second time a less disjunctive value than the first (Ps. xlii. 9).

One other use of the sign Paseq remains to be noticed. It is sometimes used with the conjunctive *Shalshéleth* to form a minor distinctive in the room of R'bhia Mugrash. If the last-named accent fall on the third word before Silluq, a minor pause may come on the second or even on the first. *Cf.* Ps. xlvii. 9, where the minor dichotomy, on the second word before Silluq, is marked by M'huppakh-Paseq. But what if the additional pause fall on the *first* word before Silluq? Can Paseq come so near the final accent as this? No, they preferred to change it into the servant Ṭarcha; and since R'bhia Mugrash can never stand before that accent, the minor distinctive, Paseq with Shalsheleth, was used as its substitute. *Cf.* Job v. 19 :—

וּבְשֵׁשַׁע ׀ לֹא־יִגַּע בְּךָ רָע׃

Yea, in seven there shall no evil touch thee.

The name *Shalshéleth* (שַׁלְשֶׁלֶת) means a "chain," and is doubtless a musical designation to indicate the succession of tones which characterised that accent. The form of its graphical sign would seem to point in the same direction. Its zigzag appearance denotes an ascending shake or trill, a modulation which brings it into the same category with Pazer. Both accents indeed are logical no less than musical. They help to bring to a successful finish the Masoretic system of notation. In the poetic, no less than in the prose accentuation, they mark the close of the dichotomy.

Examples of *Paseq-emphaticum* have been given in Chap. IX: but one or two additional illustrations from the poetical books may fitly be inserted here. *Cf.* Ps. lv. 20 :—

יִשְׁמַע ׀ אֵל ׀ וְיַעֲנֵם וְיֹשֵׁב קֶדֶם סֶלָה

The R.V. translates as a tetrastich,

> God shall hear, and answer them,
> Even he that abideth of old,   [Selah]
> *The men* who have no changes
> And who fear not God.

In this passage there are various points of
interest to the Hebrew student. We have first
the introduction of the term "Selah". This is
not strictly an integral part of the text, though
the Masoretes have accepted it as such, and
worked it into their system. It is generally regarded as a musical term indicating the place of
benedictions; and is suitably inserted after the
descriptive title or epithet which is here applied
to Jehovah. The relative אֲשֶׁר at the beginning
of the third line is rendered somewhat anomalous by its insertion, and is not easily recognised as an accusative after "hear" and
"answer". But this is no sufficient reason for
terminating the verse at the close of the first
couplet, and regarding the last two clauses as
being out of their right place. The use of two
accents on יֵשֵׁב is also to be noted. The rule is
that two servi may appear on one and the same
word, if the syllable immediately preceding the
tone be an open one. Still further we have the
meaning of the verb וַיַעֲנֵם. The A.V. has

followed the LXX in reading it as the Piel of
עָנָה "to humble or afflict," instead of the Imperf.
Qal, of עָנָה "to answer"; but this would require a
change of vowels—וִיעַנֵּם instead of וְיַעֲנֵם. It
is obvious also that the LXX must have read
וְיַעֲנֵמוֹ יֵשֵׁב in place of ויענם וישב—pointing to
a time when the undivided Hebrew text was
ויענמוישב: the termination מוֹ- being the poetical form of הֶם- as in לָמוֹ of the same verse.
This would account for the disappearance of *vav*
(=*even*) before ὁ ὑπάρχων; and shows that the
original text was not always divided in the same
way.   Finally, we have the introduction of the
double Paseq.   Dr. Kennedy thinks it enough
to say that this is a case where an unusual form
of the Divine name is marked by a pair of pointers
—a pair of note lines being required to enclose
the noteworthy form between them.   But there
is more than this.   There is the emphasis of logic
no less than of reverence.   Apart from the feeling of scrupulosity which is always associated
with the name of the Deity, there is a necessity
for the two Paseqs to indicate the importance of
the reading.   Mark the contrast between these
opening words and the rush of battle that was
raging around the righteous man in the previous

verse. There were many who strove against him; but his heart did not fear. And why? Because the heavens were not deaf. "*God* shall *hear*"—underline both words: emphasise the fact that the help of the righteous is in Jehovah —in a God who both hears and cares. Who shall say in view of this context that the insertion of a double Paseq was not necessary? The whole text suggests a twofold division:—

(1) The assured confidence of the righteous.

(2) The false confidence of the ungodly.

The former is fixed upon Jehovah, who both hears and abides forever. For in the words of Calvin, "much of that impatience into which we are hurried arises from not elevating our thoughts to the eternity of God". But the latter is based upon the fact that the wicked have no changes in the present life. Corrupted by this indulgence, they cast off all fear, and act as if they had an immunity from mortal ill. Unbroken prosperity ends in forgetfulness of God. The only other passage we shall mention is Ps. lxxiii. 28:—

> But it is *good* for me to draw near to God:
> I have made the Lord God my refuge,
> That I may tell of all thy works.

At a first reading, the LXX seems to offer a simpler and more intelligible sense, by append-

ing the words, "in the gates of the daughter of
Zion," and recasting the whole verse in the form
of a tetrastich.   The appended words, however,
are not found in any Hebrew MS.; and the
Masoretic text is not necessarily a less valuable
though a less flexible reading.   The main pause
is at *God;* for here the verse falls into two
natural divisions, dealing (1) with the assurance
that communion with God is man's chief good,
and (2) with the twofold ground on which this
confidence is based, *viz.* : that in God he has a
refuge, and that unto God he can proffer a
sacrifice of praise.   "Here is a great truth," says
Matthew Henry, "that it is good to draw near
to God: but the life of it lies in the application,
It is good for *me.*"   This is the meaning of the
emphatic Paseq (וַאֲנִי).   It enforces the contrast between the men of ver. 27, who stay "far
from God" and "perish," and the Psalmist who
has been brought to the conclusion that only in
God's presence can the heart of man find fulness
of life and joy.   Let others perish if they will,
departing from their God, but *as for me,* I will
continue stedfast in the resolution of maintain-
ing a constant fellowship with Jehovah.   The
subject then is the value and nature of divine
communion.

(1) Its value as man's supreme good.

(2) Its nature as a giving and receiving : he receives from God a refuge, and he gives to God a song.

Can it be that there is a deeper deep than this —what Zephaniah would have called a being silent in love ?   Yes.

> Thought was not : in enjoyment it expired ;
> No thanks he breathed, he proffered no request :
> Rapt into *still communion* that transcends
> The imperfect offices of prayer and praise,
> His mind was a thanksgiving to the power
> That made him : it was blessedness and love.

APPENDIX

SPECIMEN PAGE FOR STUDENT'S NOTE-BOOK

Job vii. 20.

* חָטָּאתִי מָה אֶפְעַל ׀ לָךְ֒ נֹצֵר הָאָדָ֗ם לָ֥מָה
שַׂמְתַּ֣נִי לְמִפְגָּ֣ע לָ֑ךְ וָאֶהְיֶ֖ה עָלַ֣י לְמַשָּֽׂא׃

---

* There are two forms of this interrogative particle, לָ֫מָה
which is accented on the penult (1 Sam. xix. 17) and לָמָ֫ה
before words beginning with א, ה or ע, accented on the
final syllable so as to avoid the hiatus (Gen. xxvii. 45). This
is the meaning of the Masoretic note רפה ומלעיל. The
present example is *Raphe*, without the dagesh, even though
it be *Mil'el*, *i.e.*, penultimate.

Cheyne (*Biblica*, 2472) omits the opening words as an
interpolation with Bickell and Duhm.

"Die unpoetische Form macht aber v. 20ª verdächtig,
und wahrschleinlich ist er der Ausruf eines Lesers, den der
Gedanke an Gottes Wachsamkeit und unerbittliche Strenge
erschreckte."—(Duhm.)

The A.V. reads "I have sinned; what shall I do unto thee,
O thou preserver of men?" *i.e.*, a confession. But R.V.
gives an entirely different complexion to the passage. "If
I have sinned, what do I unto thee [or, can I do], etc.?"
—(A. B. D., in *Expositor*, Oct., 1886.)

In lively speech aided by intonation almost any direct
form of expression without particles may be equivalent to
what in other languages would be conditional. *Cf.* Amos
iii. 8 : "The lion hath roared, who will not fear?" *i.e.*, *If
the lion roar*, etc.—(A. B. D., *Syntax*, p. 182.)

Often this *hypothetical perfect*, as it may be termed, is
followed by the Imperf. ἀσυνδέτως : *Have I sinned* [repeated
at xxxv. 6 with אִם : that the perfect is hypothetical is, of
course, further clear from the whole tenor of Job's argument]
what do I do to thee ?—(Driver's *Hebrew Tenses*, p. 193.)

Accents. If the dichotomy fall on the second word before
Olev'yored it is marked by Ṣinnor. In Ṣinnor's own clause,
if there be two dichotomies, the greater is marked by Pazer,
and the minor by Paseq.

εἰ ἐγὼ ἥμαρτον, τί δυνήσομαι πρᾶξαι,
 ὁ ἐπιστάμενος τὸν νοῦν τῶν ἀνθρώπων ;
διὰ τί ἔθου με κατεντευκτήν σου,
 εἰμὶ δὲ ἐπὶ σοὶ φορτίον ;

[LXX.]

א and A read δυναμαι σοι in the first line, leading Duhm to say, that it is doubtful whether it means, what *can I* do unto thee (by means of my sin) or, what *shall I* do unto thee (in the way of satisfaction for it).

This is one of the *Tiqqune Sopherim*, or improved readings of the scribes : where the LXX has still the original עָלִיךָ = επι σοι. *Cf.* Buhl's *Canon and Text*, pp. 103, 249 and Ginsburg's *Introduction*, p. 360.

In his early volume on Job, A. B. Davidson followed Ewald in taking מָה, not as interrogative, but as indefinite and Accusative to אֶפְעָל. "Be it I have sinned *in what* I owe to thee, thou watcher of men." But there is no reference to this in the *Camb. Bible*.

Watcher of men—elsewhere a word of comfort to the godly, but here used in an invidious sense to express the constant espionage exercised by God over man, that He may detect their failings.—(*Camb. Bible*.)

"O thou inspector of men" (Carey).

O Espion de l'homme (Renan).

The Hebrew accents are clearly opposed to the rendering of the A.V. "I have sinned, what, etc." A subordinate accent like Pazer does not justify so emphatic a pause at *sinned*. We must translate as the R.V. but with the emendation of the scribes :—

"If I have sinned, what can I do unto thee, O thou watcher of men ? Why hast thou set me as a mark for thee, so that I am become a burden unto thee ? "

TABLE OF ACCENTS

1. DISTINCTIVES

Prose			*Poetic*		
		PAGES			PAGES
⸺	Silluq	61	⸺	Silluq	61
⸺	Athnach	64	⸺	Olev'yored	143
⸺	S'golta	70	⸺	Athnach	64
⸺	Zaqeph	78			
⸺	Great Zaqeph	79			
⸺	Tiphcha	79			
⸺	R'bhia	80	⸺	R'bhia	80
			⸺	R'bhia Mug-	
⸺	Zarqa	103		rash	155
⸺	Pashta	95	⸺	Sinnor	103
⸺	Y'thibh	95	⸺	D'chi	80
⸺	T'bhir	98			
⸺	Geresh	107			
⸺	Gersháyim	108			
⸺	Pazer	109	⸺	Pazer	109
⸺	Great Pazer	109			
⸺	Great T'lisha	110			
⸺	Paseq	123	⸺	Paseq	123

2. CONNECTIVES

Prose	PAGES		Poetic	PAGES
⟆ Munach . .	70		⟆ Munach . .	70
⟆ M'huppakh .	96		⟆ M'huppakh .	96
⟆ Mer'kha . .	63		⟆ Mer'kha . .	63
⟆ Double				
Mer'kha .	54		⟆ Tarcha . .	80
⟆ Darga . .	99		⟆ Illuy . . .	181
⟆ Azla . . .	109		⟆ Azla . . .	109
⟆ Galgal . .	143		⟆ Galgal . .	143
⟆ Little T'lisha	110		⟆ Sinnorith .	103
			⟆ Shalshéleth .	124
				[183

INDEX OF PASSAGES

196

LIST OF TEXTS MORE FULLY TREATED
FOR THE PREACHER